PRAISE FOR MY POETS

"[A] beguiling new book . . . Genially, charismatically subversive . . .
My Poets is a delightful shock. It's also a friendly book, inviting read-
ers by its own example to let poems change them too . . . Perhaps
[poetry] makes us interesting, even beautiful, or anyway, human.
McLane's many dictions and registers, her playful digressions and
pouncing aperçus, her fast footwork that takes her from sorrow to
arch amusement in half a sentence, work to demonstrate that."

— **DAISY FRIED**, *The New York Times Book Review*

"Ms. McLane has written lyrical essays that justify the genre . . .
There's no way to convince a young person who doesn't read that in
order to have an imagination one must first seek out the imaginers,
that without them a life is less. You can only place a book in her hands
and hope for a spark. This book would do."

— **MICHAEL ROBBINS**, *The New York Observer*

"To read McLane is to be reminded that the brain may be an organ, but
the mind is a muscle. Hers is a roving, amphibious intelligence;
she's at home in the essay and the fragment, the prose note and the
elegy . . . It's a visceral kind of criticism, sexy, strange, suspense-
ful . . . McLane's personality, her laconic wit and iconoclasm, suffuse
this book . . . There is explicit autobiography here, too, painful
self-disclosure, that gives the book its emotional torque . . . Susan
Sontag called for an erotics of art. *My Poets* is that and more; it is an
erotics of epistemology."

— **PARUL SEHGAL**, *Bookforum*

"Throughout *My Poets*, her collection of beautiful, experimental essays, McLane's thinking through and appraising other poets is the central, commanding event . . . [Her] native attitude is soulful, metaphysical and witty . . . [A] gorgeous, humming collection."

—WALTON MUYUMBA, *NPR*

"[An] incandescent new collection of criticism . . . A book that may do more to change the way we think and write about poems than any since Paul Muldoon's *The End of the Poem* . . . *My Poets* is not just criticism, but art."

—MICHAEL LISTA, *National Post* (Canada)

"*My Poets* wisely avoids slapping another sales pitch on poetry. If anything, McLane shows that poetry, and the wonders within, have been ours all along."

—MICHAEL ANDOR BRODEUR, *The Boston Globe*

"McLane . . . conducts a daring experiment in *My Poets* . . . The writing . . . is exceptional throughout: vigorous, specific, and occasionally virtuosic . . . At her best, McLane is among a handful of necessary critics."

—MICHAEL AUTREY, *Booklist*

"An audacious, challenging, endearing work that defies all categorization . . . *My Poets* is at once an exuberant, even giddy, reveling in poetic fecundity and a carefully controlled and highly crafted analysis of individual poets and poems."

—PRISCILLA GILMAN, *Chicago Tribune*

"This is a vital, personal book about books . . . McLane offers openly—and brilliantly—what some critics refuse to admit: Her idiosyncrasies are her only way of reading, as mine are mine, yours yours."

—DAVE LUCAS, *The Plain Dealer* (Cleveland)

MY POETS

MAUREEN N. MᶜLANE

Maureen N. McLane is the author of
two collections of poetry, *Same Life* (FSG,
2008) and *World Enough* (FSG, 2010).
My Poets was named a finalist for the
National Book Critics' Circle Award
in Autobiography in 2012.

MY POETS

MAUREEN N. McLANE

MY POETS

FARRAR STRAUS GIROUX

NEW YORK

Farrar, Straus and Giroux
18 West 18th Street, New York 10011

Printed in the United States of America
Published in 2012 by Farrar, Straus and Giroux
First paperback edition, 2013

Portions of this book were first published, in slightly different form, in the
following publications: *Boston Review* ("My Emily Dickinson / *My Emily
Dickinson*," "My Fanny Howe"), *Modern Philology* ("My Impasses: On Not
Being Able to Read Poetry"), *Poetry* ("My Marianne Moore"), *Virginia Quarterly
Review* ("My H.D."), and *The Wallace Stevens Journal* ("My Wallace Stevens").

Owing to limitations of space, all acknowledgments for permission to
reprint previously published material can be found on pages 269–73.

The Library of Congress has cataloged the hardcover edition as follows:
McLane, Maureen N.
    My poets / Maureen N. McLane. — 1st ed.
        p. cm.
    ISBN 978-0-374-21749-5 (alk. paper)
        1. McLane, Maureen N. 2. Poets, American—Biography. 3. Poetry—
Influence. 4. Poetry—History and criticism. 5. Poetry. I. Title

PS3613.C5687 Z46 2012
811'.6—dc22
[B]

2011041208

Paperback ISBN: 978-0-374-53383-0

www.fsgbooks.com
www.twitter.com/fsgbooks • www.facebook.com/fsgbooks

1 3 5 7 9 10 8 6 4 2

Publication of this book has been aided by grants from the
Abraham and Rebecca Stein Faculty Publication Fund of New York
University, Department of English, and from the Humanities
Initiative New York University for a Grant-in-Aid award.

IN MEMORY OF BOPR, 1996–2011

SWEETEST BOY,

SWEETEST "SPIRIT OF THE AIR":

"For every house is incomplete without him
and a blessing is lacking in the spirit."

Oh! there are spirits of the air.

(PERCY BYSSHE SHELLEY)

I cannot paint / What then I was.

(WILLIAM WORDSWORTH,

"TINTERN ABBEY")

What I am saying now isn't said by me.

(OSIP MANDELSTAM, "HE WHO

FINDS A HORSESHOE")

Let me indulge the American habit of quotation:

(EZRA POUND, LETTER TO

WILLIAM CARLOS WILLIAMS)

CONTENTS

1. PROEM IN THE FORM OF A Q&A

3

2. MY CHAUCER/KANKEDORT

7

3. MY IMPASSES: ON NOT
BEING ABLE TO READ POETRY

13

4. MY ELIZABETH BISHOP/(MY GERTRUDE STEIN)

26

5. MY WALLACE STEVENS

54

6. MY WILLIAM CARLOS WILLIAMS

57

7. MY MARIANNE MOORE

69

8. MY H.D.

109

9. MY TRANSLATED: AN ABECEDARY

148

10. MY LOUISE GLÜCK

152

11. MY FANNY HOWE

175

12. MY POETS I: AN INTERLUDE
IN THE FORM OF A CENTO

186

13. MY EMILY DICKINSON/*MY EMILY DICKINSON*

193

14. MY SHELLEY/(MY ROMANTICS)

205

15. MY POETS II: AN ENVOI
IN THE FORM OF A CENTO

243

Works Consulted or Remembered and Further Reading

255

My Acknowledgments

265

MY POETS

PROEM IN THE
FORM OF A Q&A

How long have you written poetry?
   Since then—'tis Centuries—and yet
   Feels shorter than the Day
   I first surmised the Horses' Heads
   Were toward Eternity—

Why do you read poetry?
   I caught this morning morning's minion.

Why do you read poetry?
   Batter my heart.

Why do you read poetry?
   I have wasted my life.

Why do you read poetry?

> Milton! Thou shouldst be living at this hour!

What is the first poem you remember?

> She sailed away one sunny summer day
> on the back of a crocodile . . .

And then?

> 'Twas brillig, and the slithy toves
> Did gyre and gimble in the wabe.

And then?

> Anyone lived in a pretty how town . . .

And then?

> The great light cage has broken up in the air,
> freeing, I think, about a million birds.

And then?

> I sang in my chains like the sea.

Why poetry?

> Where there is personal liking we go.

Why poetry?

> Poetry sheds no tears "such as Angels weep," but natural

and human tears; she can boast of no celestial Ichor that distinguishes her vital juices from those of prose; the same human blood circulates through the veins of them both.

Why poetry?
Poetry is connate with the origin of man.

Why poetry?
Of all things of thought, poetry is closest to thought.

Why poetry?
The immortal Mind craves objects that endure.

Why poetry?
The poem is sad because it wants to be yours, and cannot.

Why poetry?
We've lived quietly among the stars, knowing money isn't what matters.

Why poetry?
A day is not a day of mind
Until all lifetime is repaired despair.

Why poetry?
                                        . . . since
our knowledge is historical, flowing, and flown.

Why poetry?
    A need for poetry.

Why do you write poetry?
    I am a native in this world
    And think in it as a native thinks.

Why do you write poetry?
    Because existence is willy-nilly thrust into our hands, our
    fate is to make something—if nothing else, the shape cut by
    the arc of our lives.

Why do you write poetry?
    Odi et amo.

Why do you write poetry?
    My purpose here is to advance into
    the sense of the weather.

Why do you write poetry?
    I sing to use the Waiting.

2.

MY CHAUCER/ KANKEDORT

I.M. JULIA BRIGGS

Was Troilus nought in a kankedort?
Chaucer, *Troilus and Criseyde*, II. 1752

Isolate, peculiar, rare, obsolete, it surfaces in the language only once, according to the latest edition of the *Oxford English Dictionary*: in Chaucer's *Troilus and Criseyde*. "Kankedort": speculatively defined as a "difficult situation" by Larry D. Benson, editor of *The Riverside Chaucer*; further glossed in the *OED* as "a state of suspense; a critical position; an awkward affair."

A lonely word whose definition can be inferred only from its single, immediate context in Chaucer's poem: Troilus awaits his beloved, Criseyde, who is being led by her uncle Pandarus to Troilus's room for their first love-meeting. Pandarus—who throughout the poem behaves like unto his name, serving as pander, go-between, near-pimp of Criseyde. Here, at the very end of Book II, the lovesick Troilus awaits his long-sought love and nervously considers how to declare his passion:

> And was the firste tyme he shulde hire preye
> Of love; O mighty God, what shal he seye?
>
> (II.1756–57)

Was Troilus nought in a kankedort? Was he not at a difficult, critical moment, that abyssal moment before erotic disclosure? Was he not worrying about the right words to say, the right words to elicit the right response, the lover's answering love, the body perhaps then pledged, then possessed? It's only humans as far as we know who can use words to get bodies together. The word as the body evanesced in a breath, a breath bearing intelligible sound. *What shal he seye?* What does he say?

> Lo, the alderfirste word that hym asterte
> Was, twyes, "Mercy, mercy, swete herte!"
>
> (III.97–98)

"Language is fossil poetry," Emerson declared in his essay "The Poet" (1844); some poetry becomes the amber in which the delicate fossils of a language are embedded. *Was Troilus nought in a kankedort?*

•

"A dream of a common language," Adrienne Rich imagined, a difficult dream. *Kankedort* falls out of this dream. Words become obsolete, languages die, texts the tombs of the dead only some learn to reanimate. Kankedort: A *hapax legomenon*, to invoke a technical term of the Greek grammarians, themselves interested especially in those words that appeared only once in the Homeric corpus. *Kankedort* a *hapax* in Chaucer's *Troilus and Criseyde* but also in the English language itself. The *OED* marks *kankedort* as not only rare but obsolete.

You find yourself in a "difficult situation."

You're asked to choose a word that has meant something to you, an invitation that lends itself to thoughts of the exceptional word, the unusual word, of a word that lodged itself like a mystery, a word that gathered around it associations so personal and ramifying that the word itself becomes the sign of an epoch not only in Troilus's life but in yours. There are words that the dictionary deems "rare," "obsolete," "slang," "obscene": lexicographers can debate such classifications and have. There are words that are "rare" for the general and words that are "rare" for you, words that are "obsolete" in the language and those that are "obsolete" for you: "Christian"; "fuckwad"; "wife." That your mind runs this way, running aground on the reef of "kankedort," of "dulcarnoun" (*Troilus and Criseyde*, III.931), of "spatchcocked," "onomastics," and other such shoals, shows your tendency toward verbal fetishism, or more precisely lexical fetishism: one could ponder the depths of the commonest words—"thing," or "think" (as Wordsworth does, incessantly); "love," "kind" (see Shakespeare); the overwhelming power encoded in the humblest parts of speech, prepositions or articles, through which every basic relation shines forth. *On. With. Together. Toward. Between. The the* (Wallace Stevens).

To focus on the word is to focus on "a part of speech"; yet no one I know ever spontaneously spoke the word "kankedort." Perhaps only Chaucer himself ever spoke the word "kankedort." He was charting his way through one of the four major dialects then jostling for the privilege of ascending into a more standard "Englysshe": Chaucer's "Englysshe" will beat out John Gower's, and that of the *Ancrene Wisse*, and other fourteenth-century variants then available on the island of Britain. If you concentrate, you can almost read Chaucer without a gloss, even if contemporary "English"—whatever that might be—is your only language.

what shal he seye?

What should I say of kankedort other than the word constellates a time, a time of reading, a time of slow dawning and changing, of delicate then desperate realizing over many months and belatedly that I was in a *kankedort*; I was sick with love; I was in love with another; I knew not what to do; I did almost nothing; I found myself *at dulcarnoun*, at my *wittes end*; I almost did something bold; I didn't; then I did; then the plot changed, or its true drift was revealed—if only in retrospect.

> *Myn owen swete herte.*
> *Kankedort.*

The harsh Teutonic consonants surfacing amid Chaucer's romance syllables, his rhyme words more typically the elegant courtly polysyllables of a Norman French: *mischaunce*; *purveiaunce*; *daliance. Kankedort* seems to leave Romance languages behind, calling up that other register of an emergent English, drawing upon Anglo-Saxon and other Germanic wells. It is striking that when Criseyde later finds herself *at . . . wittes end*, in a dilemma, she invokes a technical term from medieval Latin, itself derived from Arabic: *I am . . . at dulcarnoun*, she declares—*dulcarnoun* a term that seems to arise from a crux in geometry. It was always mixing, appropriating, bedeviling, this *Englysshe.*

The woman with whom I read *Troilus and Criseyde* and through whom I discovered *kankedort* died recently; she is beyond worldly care; I could hope that like Troilus her

> . . . lighte goost ful blissfully is went
> Up to the holughnesse of the eighthe spere
>
> (V. 1808–1809)

but that such metaphysics would falsify what I took to be her enthusiastic embrace of this single palpable world. After his death Troilus is *stellified*—that is, he is turned into a star, circling in the heavens, now stoic, now amazed to ponder human folly:

> And in hymself he lough right at the wo
> Of hem that wepten for his deth so faste.
>
> (V. 1821–1822)

Before she died she told a friend she planned to return as an owl. I can imagine her like Troilus surveying *this litel spot of erthe*, though she would be willing, unlike Troilus, to perch on merely earthly branches.

3.

MY IMPASSES

ON NOT BEING ABLE TO READ POETRY

In 1985 I took two poetry classes. I was a freshman in college and signed up for a class Professor Helen Vendler was offering (and still does) in the core curriculum: "Poems, Poets, Poetry." This was a large lecture class of some three-hundred-plus students; never did I meet Vendler (that is, until many years later). I also took a required freshman writing class, the dreaded expository writing ("Expos"); I signed up for a poetry section taught by the poet, memoirist, and art critic William Corbett.

> Two roads diverged in a yellow wood . . .
> I have been faithful to both in my fashion.

With Vendler things were clear, if intricate, sailing: the poems were rigged tight, perfect vessels expertly anthologized under the Norton name, beautifully read in her beautiful voice, three poems per class illuminated, the light of her intelligence shining through them, drawing their movements on the surface of the receptive mind. What I recall: her reading of Keats's "To Autumn," the way the numerous gnats are still descending in her voice; her reading of Yeats's "The Circus Animal's Desertion," the sublime descent into the foul rag and bone shop of the heart; her patient unweaving and reweaving of the brilliant sorrowful virtuosic strands of Milton's "Lycidas"; her casual but incisive way with a line, a fact, an insight. Who knew that funeral customs included the strewing of flowers, that "photograph" could be etymologized as light-writing, that this was a point of entry into Lowell's "Epilogue"? One understood that Vendler was remote from Pound, friendly to Eliot; that she adored Donne and Keats and Yeats and humored Allen Ginsberg like a kindly aunt; that she revered Lowell and Bishop, who had been her friends; that a rose in English smelled and sounded and sang like no rose in any other language. *Ther is no rose of swych vertu.* Poetry was untranslatable, unparaphrasable, and yet each week she accomplished before us virtuosic paraphrases. There was the thing itself, the poem compellingly read; there was a pause; and there was analysis— a dwelling on, a dwelling in, the fairer house than prose.

If Vendler's course represented the apogee of a certain form of exegesis, William Corbett's high-voltage poetry course quickly revealed the limits of close reading, or at least of my close readings.

Let us broaden the frame.

If it's true that a poem can plausibly sustain and indeed survive several interpretations, it is also true that a poem may elicit any number of bad readings.

I can tell from my misgivings when listening to some students' interpretations of poems, or when revisiting my own readings or those of some critics, that in some precinct of my mind I retain the fantasy of the Platonic reading of a poem, against which all instantiated readings are mere shadows flickering on our shared, half-illumined cave. At other times, possessed of the urge to shout "That's just wrong! Wrong Wrong Wrong!" I have had to wonder whether I don't secretly harbor a scientist's—or at least a Popperian's—view of the matter, treating critical readings as verifiable and falsifiable hypotheses.

There are many ways of *not getting it*. And many ways of *getting it* can look, years or decades or centuries later, like a symptomatic way of *not getting it*.

How could they *not have gotten* Blake? Or Dickinson? Or Stein?

Most didn't, and now some do. What happened?

One could offer numerous literary-historical, cultural, and institutional reasons for such developments, in all their specificity, and scholars have done so. What we can also say is that certain works become readable (or newly or differently readable) under certain conditions; they take up their place not exactly "in the true," as Michel Foucault describes the epistemic reconfiguration of the human sciences, but rather "in the readable," which is to say the receivable.

I am fascinated by that threshold where one hovers, not getting it yet wanting to get it. Where a tentative desire contends with frustration. Where frustration may be converted into desire, and desire into some provisional illumination. As a poet, as a student, as a critic, as a teacher, as a citizen, I have found this vale of unknowing yet wanting-to-know to be a fruitful vale, a dwelling place worth sharing, pondering. This uncomfortable yet not completely unpleasurable affective and cognitive situation presents itself to me as a somatic condition that feels rather like an environment—a kind of tensed haze. *I no sooner felt than I sought to understand* (Coleridge).

Many of the poets and poems now important to me were completely and maddeningly elusive when I first encountered them.

The shock of the new is not only a modernist mantra or an art-historical slogan but an ever-present potential charge, if you are a teacher, a student, a baby, or peculiarly receptive to opportunities for derangement.

When as a college freshman I signed up for Corbett's expository writing course, I thought I was heading for safe harbor, the heaven-haven of conventional exegesis. I would read some new poems, maybe revisit a few I knew and deepen my understanding of them. I would scan the lines, grapple with forms, wrestle with conceits, hunt down allusions, unpack metaphors, and be on the lookout for ironies. I was ready.

On Day One I was confronted with:

1

What does not change / is the will to change.

He woke, fully clothed, in his bed. He
remembered only one thing, the birds, how
when he came in, he had gone around the rooms
and got them back in their cage, the green one first,
she with the bad leg, and then the blue,
the one they had hoped was a male

Otherwise? Yes, Fernand, who had talked lispingly of Albers
    & Angkor Vat.
He had left the party without a word . . .

(CHARLES OLSON, "THE KINGFISHERS")

What?? Whaaa?

What was that crazy line break in the first line, that rene-
gade punctuation? Who was "he"? and Fernand? Albers?
Angkor Vat? And how was I going to scan those lines? What
was the form? And what was with the French and Italian
quoted later in the poem? And Mao—?? Cioa-coatl?? Where
were we? Where were we going?

On Day Two I was confronted with:

> It is 12:20 in New York a Friday
> three days after Bastille day, yes
> it is 1959 and I go get a shoeshine

because I will get off the 4:19 in Easthampton
at 7:15 and then go straight to dinner
and I don't know the people who will feed me

(FRANK O'HARA, "THE DAY LADY DIED")

Among the things I didn't know:

- that trains run on daily schedules and may be referred to
   by their time of departure
- who Lady Day was
- who Billie Holiday was
- who Bonnard was, who Mike was, what Strega was, who Mal
   Waldron was

(all mentioned in the headlong rush of the poem)

I had little idea what to do with Olson, even less (perhaps surprisingly) with O'Hara.

I could "read" these poems but I could not *read* these poems.

"It seems that a reader can only read the texts that say what he already knows." So Frances Ferguson puts it in her essay "Coleridge and the Deluded Reader."

And thus confounded I did what people do—resorted to the code-breaking tactics I knew, in this case rudimentary close-reading skills, in order to make some sense out of these two poems, which were to me at the time two equally mystifying yet somehow compelling instances of nonsense.

This was in part a case of bringing the wrong tools for the job.

It is important to observe that however different their textures, techniques, tones, conjured life-worlds, etc., these poems were alike to me in that I felt I could read neither of them. O'Hara and Olson occupy different wings of the mid- to late-twentieth-century House of American Poetry (though both are claimed for "experimental" or "oppositional" genealogies, and have been diversely anthologized as "postmoderns"), but I did not know that, and they were to me at first equally impenetrable. Olson's ostentatious and idiosyncratic erudition proved an easier zone to mine for an academically disposed reader: one could approach the text as a Poundian collage (though I wouldn't have put it this way then), as culturo-poetic critique, and could get at the component parts, even if synthesis eluded. One could at least shore up the fragments even if the meaning of the ruins escaped—though Olson's penchant for critical cultural statement did help one come up with some provisional paraphrases about the etiolation of Western civilization. The heavy, almost Teutonic intonations of Olson I could begin to hear, or so I thought. This was almost official! I could go to the library to *figure things out*.

With O'Hara, no such strategy seemed to work. Here were no literary allusions I could discern (though offhand cultural references abounded), no incorporated texts or quotations, no metaphors, no symbols, no pattern of imagery. O'Hara worked in a register of quicksilver tonal shifts whose irony and pathos I could not hear. The ebullience I got, the torque not. The mad love for jazz, painters, paintings; for New York;

for breezy urban itineraries; for friends—that's not what poetry did, what poetry held, for me. I had intimations of camp in life, not yet in literature. I had seen more blades of grass than cement.

I have the poetry anthologies we used that year; to return to them, with their penciled, painstakingly bubble-written marginalia, is to revisit not only a prior self but a prior reading self—which for me, as for many whose subjectivities were formed in dialogue with literature, have long been close to identical.

I cannot paint / What then I was (Wordsworth, "Tintern Abbey").

But I can show you a representative page, the graffiti of a prior reading moment: See opposite. These markings trace not so much the path of reading but a path of not-reading, a series of failed attempts, graspings, and gropings. In short: I cannot believe what an idiot I was!

And yet of course I can.

I was an *idiot* in the obsolete, speculative sense remarked by the *Oxford English Dictionary*:

1. b. *spec.* A layman. *Obs.*
    c. One not professionally learned or skilled; also, a private (as opposed to a public) man. *Obs.*

On first reading, I was plunged into my own private idiot Idaho; I had yet to share in the relevant communal sense-making procedures (the horizon of expectation, the interpre-

THE DAY LADY DIED

[handwritten: location in space + time]

It is 12:20 in New York a Friday
three days after Bastille day, yes *[handwritten: upheaval]*
it is 1959 and I go get a shoeshine
because I will get off the 4:19 in Easthampton
at 7:15 and then go straight to dinner
and I don't know the people who will feed me *[handwritten: isolation state]*

[handwritten right margin: lack of emotion in urban surroundings > programmed life]

I walk up the muggy street beginning to sun
and have a hamburger and a malted and buy
an ugly NEW WORLD WRITING to see what the poets *[handwritten: quasi-comical]*
in Ghana are doing these days *[handwritten: not US]*

.   I go on to the bank
and Miss Stillwagon (first name Linda I once heard)
doesn't even look up my balance for once in her life
and in the GOLDEN GRIFFIN I get a little Verlaine
for Patsy with drawings by Bonnard although I do
think of Hesiod, trans. Richmond Lattimore or
Brendan Behan's new play or *Le Balcon* or *Les Nègres*
of Genet, but I don't, I stick with Verlaine *[handwritten: indecision]*
after practically going to sleep with quandariness

[handwritten right margin: Actual journey thru the streets; is not sure; unexpected; art-trite]

and for Mike I just stroll into the PARK LANE
Liquor Store and ask for a bottle of Strega and
than I go back where I came from to 6th Avenue
and the tobacconist in the Ziegfeld Theatre and
casually ask for a carton of Gauloises and a carton
of Picayunes, and a NEW YORK POST with her face on it *[handwritten: surprise,]*

and I am sweating a lot by now and thinking of
leaning on the john door in the 5 SPOT
while she whispered a song along the keyboard
to Mal Waldron and everyone and I stopped breathing

[handwritten right margin: as her death is shock; 1st real emotion]

[handwritten: abrupt end; form = content]

[handwritten: ambiguous intention]

[handwritten bottom left: Billie Holiday]

tive community, what have you) that would make this text readable.

One must be gentle with one's former self, one's students, one's current muddles, with anyone honestly trying but not getting it.

For it would seem I did not get O'Hara at all. There is a profoundly idiot-savant quality to my marginalia, proving (yet again) the dangers of knowing a little. Re: Bastille day: "upheaval," I noted. Re: Ghana: "not US," I observed.

Yet it seems I registered something significant about the final stanza when O'Hara is stopped dead (so to speak) by "a NEW YORK POST with her face on it," the tabloid announcing Holiday's death—and the poem veers into a neo-Wordsworthian spot-of-time, a memory here cast in the perpetual undying *sweating, leaning, breathing* participial present. Here we have eulogy and lyric arrest:

> and I am sweating a lot by now and thinking of
> leaning on the john door in the 5 SPOT
> while she whispered a song along the keyboard
> to Mal Waldron and everyone and I stopped breathing

In my marginalia appended to the last line, and in a few other glosses, one discerns the trace of a new-critical vocabulary repeatedly struggling with the feeling-tone and force of the poem. The penciled "ambiguous" registers the grammatical ambiguity of the last line, *everyone* both indirect object of Holiday's whispering

> she whispered . . . / to Mal Waldron and everyone

and communal compound subject of lyric arrest:

> and everyone and I stopped breathing

I registered this ambiguity as "intentional"; I had clearly internalized the William Empson still hovering in the air, and despite warnings about the intentional fallacy, I was always looking for the poet's shaping mind and hand, particularly as inscribed in grammar and syntax. Intentional ambiguity: jackpot! And I seemed to have concluded that this abrupt end revealed an equation between form and content: the momentum bringing us to "stopped breathing"—its unpunctuated close; its refusal of a period, a full stop; the time in the poem and the time of the poem suspended—

While I did not understand this poem, I wanted to understand this poem.

I no sooner felt than I sought to understand.

And more illuminating than all my deciphering strategies, whether well or badly mustered, was Corbett's *reading* of this and other poems that semester. Here his pedagogy if not his taste was close to Vendler's—for in their respective voices, their cadences, emphases, passions, and modulations, the poems came alive, however opaque their meanings might have been.

Q: How to read?

A: ALOUD.

Q: What to do?

A: LISTEN to aficionados read those poems or works they are committed to. Some revelation will surely be forthcoming.

This is not to lapse into the fetish of "voice" or "presence" that can dominate much discussion, critical and otherwise, of poetry, but rather to keep alive a sonic dimension through which critical intelligence might also sound forth.

Q: What to do?

A: Go on the radio, do a podcast, upload a video—read and talk about a few poems.

For as Corbett proved week after week, one could learn a lot about poems, and about the impact of poetry, by osmosis. His passion and knowledge about Abstract Expressionism, specific painters, jazz musicians, networks of friends, Poundian aesthetics illuminated our reading as much as his invocation of Williams's dictum "No ideas but in things." And his specific readings of poems were, like Vendler's, live realizations of embodied understandings of specific poems.

Through a medium a message.

Damn your taste, I would like if possible to sharpen your perceptions, after which your taste can take care of itself (Pound, "Prefatio").

BACK TO THE FUTURE: OR, STILL LEARNING TO READ

I return to these early impasses in reading not simply to indulge in autobiographical meanderings but rather to suggest the important function of impasse in experience. For where my understanding failed and my rudimentary critical tools broke down, I was forced to reckon with the *impensé* of my relation to poetry. To make visible my presumptions: this is what breakdowns and impasses allowed.

I also return to these poems to trace the path and power of return; for it was precisely these and other elusive poems that bore within them a promise to me as a poet, and to me as another, future, returning reader. A reader who might get it or not get it in a new way, and who might be able to articulate the grounds for understanding, misunderstanding, and ultimately judgment.

"Not the poem which we have *read*, but the poem to which we *return*, with the greatest pleasure, possesses the genuine power, and claims the name of *essential poetry*" (Coleridge, *Biographia Literaria*).

And so:

4.

MY ELIZABETH BISHOP/
(MY GERTRUDE STEIN)

My Elizabeth Bishop begins with Gertrude Stein.

This is not usual.

Bishop is unusual but not in the way Stein is unusual.

I was not used to Gertrude Stein and found I could not get used to Stein though I tried.

I was struggling to find a topic for my undergraduate thesis.

This seemed the most important thing in the world.

Whatever is the world to you is the most important thing to you.

I would be making myself in this thing.

I was always making myself or being made.

This was unavoidable.

I was planning to be made by Gertrude Stein but she was not cooperating.

She was operating on another plane a fractured cubist grid I could not make out.

I was falling off the edge of Gertrude Stein and there was no ledge for me no stone to stand on in Gertrude Stein.

At that time.

Why did I want to be made by Stein.

She is of course very fine. Everyone thinks so except those who don't and many don't.

She is of course ridiculous until she's not and then she both is and is not ridiculous and what is ridiculous looks like something else completely.

None of this I knew then.

That was a different when.

Then I had read *Three Lives* and maybe a poem or two, "A Valentine to Sherwood Anderson" and a sweet sweet sweet sweet sweet "Susie Asado" Do.

A usual understanding was not demanded.

I thought I could make Stein mine. I thought I would make a valentine my own thesis on Gertrude Stein.

And then I read Stein or other Stein and found I could not find through Stein a line much less a through-line.

• • • •

It was summer.

Depression is much worse in summer the sun gloats.

It is summer and it is rainy and depression's gone.

Then summer had me abed anxious to find what I could find in Stein to make mine or to be made by.

I could find nothing in Stein and my mind would not be mine.

It was not mine but neither was it Stein's.

On my desk a book *Elizabeth Bishop: The Complete Poems, 1927–1979*.

Elizabeth Bishop outlived Gertrude Stein. She wrote many fewer lines.

This book is inscribed with loving lines by my friend and then-tutor Janice Knight.

Janice was a knight who shone.

A Knight-errant did not err in sending me to Elizabeth Bishop.

Elizabeth is my mother's name and this is likely not irrelevant.

Bishop was no bishop but may have known some. She seems Episcopalian.

My mother was a King Elizabeth King and Kings outrank Bishops as Shakespeare proves.

Harold Bloom claims Shakespeare invented the human and Gertrude Stein wrote *Everybody's Autobiography*.

It is a wonderful book and had I read it that sungloating summer I might never have made my move to Bishop.

A Knight in shining armor led me to Bishop and the Bishop seemed to shine more clearly than the stony Stein I could not find my way through to be made by.

For women can be Knights like Britomart cross-dressed in Spenser braving her test *Be bold*, *Be not too bold*.

Thus I came to Bishop.

• • • •

Bishop seemed an easier test than Stein.
I thought I could read Bishop and could know that mind and
    make it mind my mind.
There was clear sense in such lines and outlines—

> Land lies in water; it is shadowed green.

There was a neat conceit and epigrams to diagram.

> Topography displays no favorites; North's as near as West.
> More delicate than the historians' are the map-makers' colors.
>
> ("THE MAP")

And now I remember what I did not remember when I started
    my thesis on Gertrude Stein become Elizabeth Bishop—

> The art of losing isn't hard to master

Before the gift of a Knight there was an earlier one, one Caro-
    line Fraser who has written since of rewilding the world
    and of a Mormon massacre who at that time brought into
    class a villanelle about a muffled hell that rhymed so well
    it carved its lines on soul:

> The art of losing isn't hard to master;
> so many things seem filled with the intent
> to be lost that their loss is no disaster.

Lovely Caroline who seemed somehow depressed and depressed with us blank freshmen brought us into this disaster, this master, this losing and frenzy of possessed dispossession that haunted us after.

So before I lost my mind in Gertrude Stein and found my way to Bishop I had found a way into Bishop by losing her way in disaster.

Elizabeth Bishop was a master who would not play master.

Gertrude Stein was a master she declared *Einstein was the creative philosophic mind of the century and I have been the creative literary mind of the century / I know that I am the most important writer writing today* and this time I think Stein was fine and right to say so though she's flayed so for saying so.

Alice B. Toklas was master in bed to the dread of Hemingway who stumbled on their love play.

It ruined his day.

This made my day.

What Bishop did in bed is something left unsaid until it's said or somewhat said (as in an unpublished poem published only long after she was dead):

> In a cheap hotel
> in a cheap city
> Love held his prisoners . . .
> . . . .
> Almost every night   —frequently

> [every night] he drags me
> back to that   bed
> the ice clinks, the fan whirs.
> He chains me & berates me—
> He chains me to that bed & he berates me.
>
> ("IN A CHEAP HOTEL . . .")

Her blood ran red as a bullfighter's dead in the ring his cape
    spread under his head.
Her blood ran red as Hemingway's in another way.
She like him fished in the Florida Keys. But did they let every
    fish go I do not think so.

● ● ● ●

Everybody likes Elizabeth Bishop because she is nice.
Elizabeth Bishop will not cut off your nuts or bare her vagina.
She could though make a rose a rose a rose—

> . . . roses, roses, roses,
> exacting roses from the body,
> and the even darker, accurate, rose of sex—

—in a not so vague "Vague Poem (Vaguely Love Poem)" which
    Bishop herself did not publish during her lifetime: cf. the
    vagaries of publishing unpublished Bishop.
Elizabeth Bishop made a queer map.

Elizabeth Bishop did not mistake the map for the territory.
She did not take territory as if that were the only story unlike
    Robert Lowell.
Robert Lowell is so Lowelly you must unLowell him to lower
    him into you.
This I found.
He was not sound.

> My mind's not right.
> . . . .
>   . . . I hear
> my ill-spirit sob in each blood cell,
> as if my hand were at its throat . . .
> ("SKUNK HOUR")

He was wound tight and then unwound. Lost, found. He got
    around.
Bishop did so famously. Her titles show a wide sightseeing,
    places for living and being—"Wading at Wellfleet," "Paris,
    7 a.m.," "Quai d'Orléans," "Florida," "Cape Breton," "Var-
    ick Street," "Arrival at Santos," "Brazil, January 1, 1502,"
    "First Death in Nova Scotia." She was *North & South*. She
    was all geography her last book *Geography III*.
Elizabeth Bishop moved on many squares. Her seas were lairs.

> We'd rather have the iceberg than the ship . . .
> ("THE IMAGINARY ICEBERG")

But he sleeps on the top of his mast
with his eyes closed tight.
The gull inquired into his dream,
which was, "I must not fall.
The spangled sea below wants me to fall.
It is hard as diamonds; it wants to destroy us all."

("THE UNBELIEVER")

"Elizabeth Bishop: A Study of Poetic Location" is what I called
my thesis.
It had no thesis it was largely exegesis.
This was before everyone knew Elizabeth Bishop. Before gen-
eral worship.
There were essays and fans but no biography.
There was Ashbery.
She was hard to see.
Her letters were in Houghton Library.
Her letters to Robert Lowell.
Bishop was an American poet in Brazil while Lowell was an
American poet in America.
He was official. His private was public. He was privy to our
public republic.
He had a wide mind but not so deep as Bishop who sounded
seas—

Cold dark deep and absolutely clear,
element bearable to no mortal . . .

("AT THE FISHHOUSES")

She is sometimes and rarely erotic. Lowell was manic, scle-
  rotic. His letters to her were not in Houghton Library.
One side of a correspondence is a thing to see.
The librarians insisted on pencil.
Houghton surely knew Lowells who spoke only to Cabots who
  spoke only to God.
Harvard was Harvard is Harvard Harvard.
Boston was a microcosm of provincial orgasm taking itself for
  world cataclysm.
Bishop had a different prism.

● ● ● ●

I do not know thoroughly how she made me or whether did
  she.
"Usury has made us," Lowell wrote Bishop, apropos of their
  trust funds. This was honest and partial.
If you read Bishop you read Lowell and Marianne Moore you
  read a full score.
Bishop advised students to read a poet wholly through and all
  his work letters too.
Keats was her giant. Lowell was not Keats.
A hundred poems more or less. One hundred poems to read
  and discuss and express.
In my book of Knight's heraldry are marks of significancy. I
  circled the titles that sang to me.

Elizabeth Bishop was gay and a traveler and a gay and sad traveler.

I did not know this and I came to know this.

I became this.

Elizabeth Bishop was an orphan asthmatic alcoholic you almost never smell the alcohol on the breath of her poems.

Bishop dedicated *A Cold Spring* (1955) to her therapist Dr. Anny Baumann which was a touching gesture.

A nod to rescue.

The thing about not knowing about the life of the life of the poets you're reading is that you never know when it might start bleeding.

The thing about reading the letters of a poet trying to feel out the shape of the mind of the poet is that one day you may find a break in the poet.

In Brazil there were servants and flowers and birds and weather and architecture and Lota.

> Hidden, oh hidden
> in the high fog
> the house we live in,
> beneath the magnetic rock,
> rain-, rainbow-ridden,
> where blood-black
> bromelias, lichens,
> owls, and the lint

of the waterfalls cling,

familiar, unbidden.

("SONG FOR THE RAINY SEASON")

These appear in her letters the letters now published then
   filed in a large box in Houghton.
Servants and flowers and birds and weather and architecture
   and Lota appear in her letters and then one day no letters
   then one month no letter then later the letter where Lota's
   died by her own hand the library walls split open.

—Even losing you (the joking voice, a gesture
I love) I shan't have lied. It's evident
the art of losing's not too hard to master
though it may look like (*Write* it!) like disaster.

("ONE ART")

●   ●   ●   ●

Virginia Woolf recalled the days before the war the Great War
that Gertrude Stein also wrote about that Bishop also wrote
about in "In the Waiting Room" that before the war poets used
to sing together in the mind: before the war one hummed un-
der one's breath at luncheon parties. Alfred Tennyson and
Christina Rossetti hummed together in the mind. In *A Room
of One's Own* Woolf wonders

Why has Alfred ceased to sing

> She is coming, my dove, my dear?

Why has Christina ceased to respond

> My heart is gladder than all these

> Because my love is come to me?

Shall we lay the blame on the war? When the guns fired in
August 1914, did the faces of men and women show so plain
in each other's eyes that romance was killed? . . . But lay
the blame where one will, on whom one will, the illusion
which inspired Tennyson and Christina Rossetti to sing so
passionately about the coming of their loves is far rarer
now than then. One has only to read, to look, to listen, to
remember.

One may not have so many luncheon parties to remember as
Woolf had to remember but one may still remember a war one
never experienced a war may make itself felt in an absence of
humming. And still yet still there is a humming still thrum-
ming in the ears when sometimes Elizabeth Bishop and Mar-
ianne Moore sing together in the mind, when Marianne
swings in—

> Where there is personal liking we go.
>
> ("THE HERO")

and Elizabeth declares—

We'd rather have the iceberg than the ship,
although it meant the end of travel.

("THE IMAGINARY ICEBERG")

and Elizabeth announces:

We must admire her perfect aim,
this huntress of the winter air.

("THE COLDER THE AIR")

Or when Marianne confides—

My father used to say,
"Superior people never make long visits,
have to be shown Longfellow's grave
nor the glass flowers at Harvard."

("SILENCE")

and Bishop responds:

My grandfather said to me
as we sat on the wagon seat,
"Be sure to remember to always
speak to everyone you meet."

("MANNERS")

And sometimes Bishop and Lowell chime together in the
mind, as when Robert recalls:

I was five and a half.
My formal pearl gray shorts
had been worn for three minutes.
My perfection was the Olympian
poise of my models in the imperishable autumn
display windows
of Rogers Peet's boys' store below the State House
in Boston. Distorting drops of water
pinpricked my face in the basin's mirror.
I was a stuffed toucan
with a bibulous, multicolored beak.

("MY LAST AFTERNOON WITH
UNCLE DEVEREUX WINSLOW")

And Elizabeth replies:

In the cold, cold parlor
my mother laid out Arthur
beneath the chromographs:
Edward, Prince of Wales,
with Princess Alexandra,
and King George with Queen Mary.
Below them on the table
stood a stuffed loon
shot and stuffed by Uncle
Arthur, Arthur's father.

("FIRST DEATH IN NOVA SCOTIA")

Or when Elizabeth sings from Brazil:

> This is the time of year
> when almost every night
> the frail, illegal fire balloons appear.
>
> ("THE ARMADILLO")

And Robert replies from New England:

> The season's ill—
> we've lost our summer millionaire,
> who seemed to leap from an L. L. Bean
> catalogue.
>
> ("SKUNK HOUR")

and Elizabeth keens in Brazil:

> The ancient owls' nest must have burned.
> Hastily, all alone,
> a glistening armadillo left the scene,
> rose-flecked, head down, tail down,
>
> and then a baby rabbit jumped out,
> *short*-eared, to our surprise.
>
> ("THE ARMADILLO")

and Robert replies from Maine:

nobody's here—

only skunks, that search
in the moonlight for a bite to eat.

("SKUNK HOUR")

Or when Elizabeth sings to her childself:

But I felt: you are an *I*,
you are an *Elizabeth*,
you are one of *them*.
Why should you be one, too?

("IN THE WAITING ROOM")

And Jorie Graham replies:

. . . I was
sick, in bed, my first time, since beginning, since beginning
school, since the becoming of my self.
I looked for the notes but walls slid in. A weight
descended. I was waiting.

("OTHER")

● ● ● ●

Elizabeth Bishop is pre-PC.
She wrote "Songs for a Colored Singer."
This was an attempt to sing like Billie.

There is no holiday from race in any century though there are different holidays and different races in different countries.

Bishop has a poem or two about servants. She wrote "Cootchie"—

> Cootchie, Miss Lula's servant, lies in marl,
> black into white she went
>> below the surface of the coral reef.

Gertrude Stein writes about servants. Woolf did less so but depended greatly on her servants as Alison Light explores in her book *Mrs. Woolf and the Servants*.

The question of servants and poetry has yet to be fully answered. It is related but not identical to the question of women and writing, whose fires are lighting and by whom in whose rooms.

You know already what the answer might be.

There is a poetry of servants and a poetry for servants. Is this so. Is this what servants think or thought one would like to know. Servants kill masters in ballads and movies. There is a novel in the voice of Gertrude Stein's Vietnamese cook: Monique Truong's *The Book of Salt*. Gertrude Stein and Alice B. Toklas had Chinese and Vietnamese servants after French and Alsatian and Italian servants did not work out their not working out putting all in doubt:

We have Chinese servants now and sometimes the name
they say they are has nothing to do with what they are they
may have borrowed or gambled away their reference and
they seem to be there or not there as well with any name and
anyway the Oriental, and perhaps a name there is not a
name, is invading the Western world. It is the peaceful pen-
etration that is important not wars . . . We have a Chinese
servant now because alas the French servants and their
cooking is not what it was.

(EVERYBODY'S AUTOBIOGRAPHY)

Elizabeth Bishop has interesting poems about squatters and
tenants and the poor in Brazil they are not except perhaps
for "Manuelzinho" successful they are attempts and symp-
toms and nevertheless interesting.
As Stein said, "Identity always worries me and memory and
eternity."
And: "Inside and outside and identity is a great bother."
Whose inside whose outside is what one wants to know who's
and who's.

> Suddenly, from inside,
> came an *oh!* of pain
> —Aunt Consuelo's voice—
> not very loud or long.
>
> . . . .

. . . What took me
completely by surprise
was that it was *me*:
my voice, in my mouth.
Without thinking at all
I was my foolish aunt,
I—we—were falling, falling,
our eyes glued to the cover
of the *National Geographic*,
February, 1918.

. . . .

Why should I be my aunt,
or me, or anyone?

("IN THE WAITING ROOM")

As "The Gentleman of Shalott" has it: "Which eye's his eye?"
"And identity is funny being yourself is funny as you are never
    yourself to yourself except as you remember yourself and
    then of course you do not believe yourself" (Stein, *Every-
    body's Autobiography*).
You are of course never yourself.
Let me recite what history teaches. History teaches (Stein, "If I
    Told Him: A Completed Portrait of Picasso").

● ● ● ●

Jonathan Galassi loves Bishop in a real and pure way. People make friends over Bishop and enemies over Lowell. Some people say you cannot like both Stein and Bishop they line up in little teams they taunt the other teams or refuse to let them play on their field this is moronic like many a school-yard game. Not that there is not discrimination required but discriminating may yet bring you to a place where Bishop meets Stein and Stein meets Bishop and they are quite congenial and have tea in the mind. Life is surprising like that so is poetry most people do not wish to be surprised especially once they have announced their team and bought their team uniforms.

Now everyone likes Elizabeth Bishop except the ones who don't Louise Glück once said she never could see all the fuss about Bishop or she did not say so exactly but made plain that this was what she felt which was amusing and a sharp shift from the bovine worship Bishop in some quarters elicits.

For a bishop may be promoted to a pope and Bishop is not infallible.

There are several poems that if not dreadful not god-awful not even "awful but cheerful" are just dull.

Bishop like Wordsworth courts the dull.

They are suspicious of excitement which excites suspicion in ages enthralled by sensation.

Wordsworth is very very dull until you suddenly feel his way of
    being dull is the elemental vital way to be.
He sometimes then again becomes dull.
Wordsworth is inexorable Bishop is parenthetical. Her pa-
    rentheses create emphases even when their purpose is to
    hesitate not asseverate.
From first to last her parentheses proliferate—

> Icebergs behoove the soul
> (both being self-made from elements least visible)
> to see them so: fleshed, fair, erected indivisible.
>
> ("THE IMAGINARY ICEBERG")

> . . . the lines
> that we drive on (satin-stripes on harlequin's
>   trousers, tights) . . .
>
> ("FROM THE COUNTRY TO THE CITY")

> . . . watching his toes.
> —Watching, rather, the spaces of sand between them,
> where (no detail too small) the Atlantic drains
> rapidly backwards and downwards.
>
> ("SANDPIPER")

> —this little painting (a sketch for a larger one?)
> has never earned any money in its life.
>
> ("POEM")

> I wanted to get as far as my proto-dream-house,
> my crypto-dream-house, that crooked box
> set up on pilings, shingled green,
> a sort of artichoke of a house, but greener
> (boiled with bicarbonate of soda?) . . .

("THE END OF MARCH")

Some early poems are tight knots I could not then undo and may not now undo. Some knots are fine knotted.

I do not really know what "A Miracle for Breakfast" miracles.

One feels the poet seek refuge in *those blessèd structures plot and rhyme* or rather in a series of sweet conceits like Herbert or Donne did.

Metaphysic is good physic and a tonic for poets who are grown-ups or aspiring.

Some poets have minds.

Wordsworth had the egotistical sublime Keats had negative capability though in "Hart-Leap Well" or "We Are Seven" Wordsworth is as capable of negative capability as Keats or Bishop.

Gertrude Stein distinguished between the egotism of the painter and the egotism of the writer. She knew whereof she spoke.

There are so many egotisms one would need to create multiple taxons.

Bishop's parentheticals are like Moore's pangolin's scales

features essential for defense what is defended here is the possibility of exact vision which means revision which means seeing and thinking in time unfolding which may partially undo the foregoing:

As in:

> . . . we followed
> a track of big dog-prints (so big
> they were more like lion-prints).
>
> ("THE END OF MARCH")

or—

> A river schooner with raked masts
> and violet-colored sails tacked in so close
> her bowsprit seemed to touch the church
>
> (Cathedral, rather!).
>
> ("SANTARÉM")

And then there are the parentheticals that move us beyond gloss beyond what perceiving will still bear revising to the end of revising the writing of dying:

> . . . You can't derange, or re-arrange,
> your poems again. (But the Sparrows can their song.)
> The words won't change again. Sad friend, you cannot change.
>
> ("NORTH HAVEN," IN MEMORIAM: ROBERT LOWELL)

—Even losing you (the joking voice, a gesture
I love) I shan't have lied. It's evident
the art of losing's not too hard to master
though it may look like (*Write* it!) like disaster.

("ONE ART")

• • • •

There is a Chinese patience in Vermeer's craft said Proust the
last thing he said. Bishop has a kindred patience not a man-
darin's like Moore's more like a birder's who does not wish
unlike Audubon to kill the specimen.

Such a proliferation of parentheticals could become a tic be-
come a manner could seem overcorrect.

Some poems smack of a gentility one would like in some
moods to smack out of them.

Viz: The mysterious wooden structure set against the sea and
sky in "The Monument":

It is the beginning of a painting,
a piece of sculpture, or poem, or monument,
and all of wood. Watch it closely.

Viz: A small naively yet precisely painted landscape in
"Poem":

Heavens, I recognize the place, I know it!

These poems and these moments have been much praised it is something how often a poet is praised for the very thing that is a fault.

It is true one can think one thing then another thing then back one finding a poem like "The Fish" a marvel then not then again yes—the poet's slow presenting of the fish she's caught the deferred seeing of the five snapped fish lines and hooks still dangling from its "aching jaw" her slow dawning consciousness of the ancient fish's history of victorious escape the spilled gas shining in the boat's well—

> . . . —until everything
> was rainbow, rainbow, rainbow!
> And I let the fish go.

Some days this seems coercively tidy and moral and obligatorily epiphanic and another instance of romantic ideology and sickening other days it seems a parable for living or rather attending. For one cannot sustain beyond adolescence the fiction of the amorality of literature Sade was a moralist. And Shelley reminds us *the great secret of morals is love* in his "A Defence of Poetry" it is a *going out of our own nature.*

Avant-gardes are necessary and disgusting and necessary to make one disgusted with the prevailing and then with the avant-garde once it prevails.

They are always borrowing from the future to hector the now.

But remember what Ashbery says in "Self-Portrait in a Convex Mirror": "Tomorrow is easy, but today is uncharted." True it is.

It is never clear in a moment what is of a moment. Then there is a time when something seems only of that moment that moment now past and the requiem may start.

I think the requiem began long ago for Robert Lowell but has not yet for Bishop Moore or Stein. The American Century is over.

This may be merely personal there are some for whom no requiem could ever begin for Lowell who to them could never become "a stuffed toucan."

• • • •

All that summer and then fall and then winter I read Bishop though I cannot help but feel that I could not read Bishop though I read Bishop and wrote a long thesis on Bishop. I could not help but feel that for all the dwelling on the poems the poems were eluding me. They were eluding and unsettling and sometimes boring they were settling in me they bore in me.

Devin Johnston once said I do not know why they are so preoccupied with having knowledge at the University of Chicago I thought knowledge was something that passes through you not something you had.

This was orphic and wise and very unclenching unlike the
   university.
Bishop was a sea to swim in not a university though a univer-
   sity might become some years a sea.
Bishop was a sea to breathe in once the gills you needed grew
   and breathing grew less strange.
Bishop was a sea to range in to wade in to be made in.
Cold dark deep and absolutely clear—
I do not know what I know about Bishop but what I came to
   through Bishop—

> If you should dip your hand in,
> your wrist would ache immediately,
> your bones would begin to ache and your hand would burn
> as if the water were a transmutation of fire
> that feeds on stones and burns with a dark gray flame.

("AT THE FISHHOUSES")

Bishop was not Stein but she was neither *icily free above the
   stones* nor was she a *cold hard mouth* nor *all a case of knives.*
You are of course never yourself you are never sure what you
   might be made by or mind or make.
One could feed on stones one could swim in the sea one could
   rest not knowing what anything might be.
Identity always worries me and memory and eternity.

> It is like what we imagine knowledge to be:
> dark, salt, clear, moving, utterly free,

drawn from the cold hard mouth

of the world, derived from the rocky breasts

forever, flowing and drawn, and since

our knowledge is historical, flowing, and flown.

("AT THE FISHHOUSES")

5

MY WALLACE STEVENS

My Wallace Stevens is an insurgent inchling in the bristling forest and a stolid giant rolling metaphysical rhymes down the mountain.

The editors of the college yearbook asked for a quotation, a line, a phrase, something to accompany your picture.

Let be be finale of seem.

Well what is that supposed to mean? they asked.

I didn't know and I don't and I was ecstatic.

• • • •

SUMMER BEER WITH ENDANGERED GLACIER

My one eye
does not match
the other

Corrective
lenses regulate
whatever

needs require.
Seeing?
I was being

being seen.
Let be
be finale.

Let our virtues
tally
up against

the obvious.
If we
don't believe

ourselves
custodial
why all

the hoobla-
hoo, hulla-
baloo?

Passivist
mon semblable
ma soeur

soi même
blow through
this blue

6.

MY WILLIAM
CARLOS WILLIAMS

Like hundreds if not thousands of Americans before me, I
went to Europe to make myself into a writer. I would not have
put it this way then; it was too bold, too naked, too foreign, too
estranging an ambition. And it was almost submerged. But it
was there. Now hordes of young Americans go to Asia, to South
America, to Timbuktu, as casually as if they were taking off for
a weekend in Maine; and as August Kleinzahler has said, all the
real talent nowadays goes into TV and the movies. I had no
conception of making anything except a thing out of language.
It seemed to present a lower bar for entry, like jogging as op-
posed to, say, Pilates. It also answered a native longing. If I'd
been born later, or in a different place, or taken in different
things, the impulses might have moved me differently, but
there I was. It was clear I was good at school—thus the scholar-
ship to Oxford; not clear that I was a writer, or a poet. The very
things that made me good at school—a talent for aligning with

authority, or for knowing what it wanted; a capacity for self-estranging self-discipline; an ability to use anxiety as a fuel; an overidentification with established codes—were precisely the things that might render me *not a writer, not a poet*. (It was William Carlos Williams, after all, who grimly pronounced, of the American scene, *never a woman, never a poet*.) I went to England and hoped to make myself into a poet. I had written some poetry, in fits and starts, mostly execrable, some things minimally competent as imitations; nothing memorable.

> *I cannot paint / What then I was.*
> *Have you always written poetry?*

My coursework would take me from Middle English to T. S. Eliot. In college I had studied American history and literature and felt keenly the lack of any grounding in "English literature." Now I was going to submit, ecstatically, to The Tradition; I was going to read poets whenever I had the time and choice of reading; I was going to immerse myself in "the mind of Europe"; I was going to out-Eliot Eliot!

I was going to become a goddamn American poet!

I had first to become

    a. an American
    b. a poet

Perhaps I already was these.

I entered

> . . . the new world naked,
> cold, uncertain of all
> ("BY THE ROAD TO THE
> CONTAGIOUS HOSPITAL")

Going to England is a fast way to become American.

I would be *pole-axed by the poll tax*. I would watch a terrible Australian soap opera daily at noon with a shy Egyptologist. I would ponder Margaret Thatcher's helmet of hair and John Major's garden gnomes. I would hear the subjunctive deployed daily, correctly. I would play rugby, hear Scots, sing in a Bach choir. I would see Nelson Mandela walk free on TV. I would be served revolting pizza with corn toppings. I would be served pudding upon pudding. I would hear dons precisely and sometimes maliciously place their students by accent. I would discover whole new horizons of insult. I would hear the yobs and louts burst nightly out of The Kings Arms at closing time, belting their homosocial ditties at the sodden tops of their lungs. I would see how the Empire struck back, the only decent food to be found in the two Indian restaurants run by beautiful benighted Pakistanis. I would watch the late afternoon expand into beautiful languorous hours. I would be sent messages in college via *pigeon-post*. I would have a rickety bike called Winston. I would return to the States once in two years. I would call my lover once a month. I had no e-mail. I wrote letters.

William Carlos Williams's brilliant *In the American Grain* was written largely while he was aboard ship to Europe.

Yet Williams generally stayed home—though he was militantly cosmopolitan as well as militantly local and provincial (thus the epic *Paterson*, starring Paterson, New Jersey, as both city and "giant" protagonist). The "Carlos" flagged his Spanish heritage, the Puerto Rican transit of his mother's line. He Caribbeanized, mestizo-ized, hybridized American studies. Or almost might have. He laid down a track.

Like D. H. Lawrence, he was mad for Indians. Like D. H. Lawrence, he hated Puritans.

It was fashionable to hate Puritans in the 1920s.

I spent much time in the late 1980s and early 1990s studying Puritans—American Puritans in particular. They were in many ways exemplary, with their hard little souls, their rigor, their disputations, their predestinations, their agonized soul-inquiries, their inventories, their striking sensualities, their *be dead to the world but diligent in all worldly business*, their *be of the world but not in it*, their sermons organized into *texts doctrines reasons uses*, their orthodoxies, their dissidents, their antinomians, their expulsions, their John Cotton/Thomas Shepard/Anne Hutchinson/John Winthrop, their witch burnings, their companionate marriages, their City upon a Hill, their Half-Way Covenant, their sense that everything mattered at every awful moment—for one was either elect or damned and there was no flimflammery like Purgatory to set accounts to right.

And in the rigorous particulars of certain Puritan theologians, in their Calvinist *justification by faith alone*, in their theology of *grace not works*, in their combination of fear, trembling, bliss, and abjection, I found a peculiarly answering spirit, for like the English Puritan John Bunyan *I was both a burden and a terror to myself*.

For *Title Divine—is Mine!*

For *Mine—by the right of the White Election!*

For Jonathan Edwards. For Emily Dickinson. For Marilynne Robinson.

For

> My religion makes no sense
> and does not help me
> therefore I pursue it.
>
> **(ANNE CARSON,**
> **"THE TRUTH ABOUT GOD")**

For I was done (I thought) with Catholicism but seventeenth- and eighteenth-century theology still possessed an intellectual glamour. For Harvard was still mad for Puritans especially Alan Heimert intellectual son of Perry Miller and Janice Knight student of Heimert.

For Williams wrote against know-nothings and prudes and mistakenly aligned all this with Puritans: *All that will be new in America will be anti-Puritan. It will be of another root.* He despised Pilgrims: *they, the seed, instead of growing, looked black at the world and damning its perfections praised a zero in themselves.*

One could write this only if one had not truly reckoned with Jonathan Edwards—his exact, impassioned registrations of the natural world; his profoundly rigorous and mobile intellect; his alertness to developments in natural science; his beautiful homage to the young girl who would become his wife; his sensual vision of the loving embrace of the Lord in the paradise of the Elect—

● ● ● ●

One feels in Williams's longer works (*Paterson* but also the earlier *Spring and All*) and in his more discursive prose the strain of a felt, necessary polemic: against smug provincialism, against equally smug Europhilia, against expatriatism, against Boston Brahminism in literature, against the cult of Paris, against propriety, against *know-nothings*, against academics, against asceticism, against T. S. Eliot. He satirized his critics, ventriloquizing them: "You moderns! it is the death of poetry you are accomplishing" (*Spring and All*).

Whom he praised: the French explorer Samuel Champlain, "this American; a sort of radio distributor sending out sparks to us all"; Edgar Allan Poe; Marianne Moore; Gertrude Stein; Mina Loy; Montezuma; Walter Raleigh; "contact"; the NEW. *All that will be new in America will be anti-Puritan. It will be of another root*—the French, the Spanish, the Indian, the Negro.

Like Wordsworth, like Whitman, like Ginsberg, he praised "experience": *My whole life has been spent (so far) in seeking to place a value upon experience (Spring and All)*. As a physician, as a poet, he appreciated the clinical, etymological proximity of "experience" to "experiment." For all their surface difference, his best poems are like Keats's in that they are *proved on the pulse.*

There in Rutherford, New Jersey, Dr. William Carlos Williams was birthing babies *by the road to the contagious hospital* and eyeing the *young slatterns* and driving by nightgowned housewives hanging out their laundry and dancing alone in his room before his mirror the lonely god of his household and he was listening closely to the Polacks and the Elsies and the Negroes and the *banjo jazz* and the other *pure products of America.*

Pure, impure: let's be done with that.

On his romance with the Indian: "Doesn't it make you want to go out and lift dead Indians tenderly from their graves, to steal from them—as if it must be clinging even to their corpses —some authenticity . . ." (*In the American Grain*).

He praised the *rich regenerative violence* of Daniel Boone— *a great voluptuary born to the American settlements against the niggardliness of the damning puritanical tradition.* One could see this romance with violence (and with the frontier, and the Indian) as a typically American syndrome, or more broadly as a symptom of a Euro-American masculine anxiety—the inflated hypermasculine sub-Nietzschean strain here prominent throughout late-nineteenth- and early-twentieth-century cultural critique.

For William Carlos Williams it was *no ideas but in things.*

I first heard this in 1985, in a freshman poetry class.

I was like, WTF?

For I was *beauty is truth, truth beauty*; I was that *dapple-dawn-drawn Falcon*; I was *Batter my heart*; I was *the leaf, the blossom, or the bole*; I was not *a red wheel / barrow glazed with rain / water beside the white / chickens*. I was not *the plums . . . so sweet / and so cold*. I was not looking to open refrigerators in poems or to take joyrides in jagged verse. I did not care for

> . . . muddy fields
>
> brown with dried weeds, standing and fallen
>
> **("BY THE ROAD TO THE CONTAGIOUS HOSPITAL")**

I did not want to pay attention to the scrub of New Jersey. I had seen plenty of scrub; I'd had enough.

Yet though I did not know it I was certainly a *pure product of America going crazy.*

From Williams, the apparent idiot-savancy of

> *I have eaten / the plums*

of

> *so much depends.*

And damn if so much doesn't depend!—

                    upon

                    a red wheel
                    barrow

                    glazed with rain
                    water

                    beside the white
                    chickens

      So much depends
      upon
      enjambment!
      upon
      upon!—
as the preposition-mad Gertrude Stein might have put it.
      For as Robert Creeley wrote in "The Window,"

                    Position is where you
                    put it . . .

And with certain masters of technique—Williams, Creeley,
George Oppen, Gwendolyn Brooks, Lorine Nicdecker, Rae
Armantrout:

                    . . . It
                    all drops into
                    place. . . .

                    (CREELEY, "THE WINDOW")

such that a line break may shatter your skull—

> ...We
> Die soon.

(BROOKS, "WE REAL COOL")

And as James Schuyler wrote in his *Diary*, "it's the matter of where the line turns."

Schooled on Williams and Whitman and Charles Olson's *Maximus* poems (and on Keats and Yeats and Bishop), desperate to align myself with the ringing I was always hearing, eager to make the pulse in my skull a sharable surge, having come to England I made my resolve:
I would write a goddamn long American poem!
It would have Indians!
   (Didn't my maternal grandparents come from the Mohawk valley? Didn't I know something about Iroquois? Hadn't I read something about King Philip's War?)
It would have documents!
   (Didn't I know how to poke around in archives? Hadn't I put a toe in the waters of historiography? Hadn't I studied *Paterson*, jammed with bits of local lore, historical anecdotes, Alexander Hamilton's schemes, lists of rock samples, newspaper reports, excerpts from agonized letters?)
And so: to begin!
: a reply to Greek and Latin with the bare hands! (*Paterson* I).

Yet despite some mucking around in John Smith's *Generall Historie of Virginia*; despite some experiments in document-based pastiche; despite my admiration for Susan Howe's revisionary poetic-archival work; despite the sharpening of my often uneasy sense that I was indeed an American, whatever that was, this project I soon abandoned.

And that was a good thing.

For if poetry need not always *come as easily as leaves to the tree* (Keats), if it be excessively willed it becomes, for me, an abomination. And Shelley says: "Poetry is not like reasoning, a power to be exerted according to the determination of the will. A man cannot say, 'I will compose poetry.' The greatest poet even cannot say it" ("A Defence of Poetry"). We *hate poetry that has a palpable design on us*, as John Keats wrote in a letter to John Hamilton Reynolds on February 3, 1818. (Although one must worship Milton, who had nothing but designs on us—and here, once again, I am brought to say the very opposite of what I just said, as was Keats.)

In England and long after, my ideas were out of joint with my realities.

No ideas but in things.

My main project in England, as life would have it, was to read and to suffer, and I did both.

My whole life has been spent (so far) in seeking to place a value upon experience (Spring and All).

I did not know how to put a value on experience, and particularly on my experience; I did not even know how to experience my experience.

Yes as Alice Notley says

> how be what you are what's experience but
> a becoming acceptable to the keepers
> of surfaces say this University.

> ("EXPERIENCE")

To England I had come with inchoate ambitions and aspirations and nothing would go as I'd thought.

How be what you are.

And while Williams was wrong to say *The past is dead* (*Paterson*, III.iii.142), he wasn't wrong to say *Music it for yourself* (*Paterson*, I.iii.30).

And not for the first time and not for the last I was brought to see that "The Person That You Were Will Be Replaced" (Notley).

And it would be a long while before I might venture to think—

> So glad I don't have to write
> in the styles of the poetries I was taught
> they were beautiful and unlike me
> positing a formal, stylized woman.
> But I am the poet, without doubt.
> Experience is a hoax.

> (NOTLEY, "EXPERIENCE")

7.

MY MARIANNE MOORE

Of her creatures much has been written—the jerboa, the pangolin, the monkeys, the snails, the ostrich or "camel-sparrow"; the bristles, the shells, the scales, the probes, the reticulate defenses. Of her syllabics, much. Of her intricate structures, collaged facts, tonal severities, occasional whimsies, impish arrivals. Of her singular modernism. Of her tricorn hat; her Brooklyn residence with her formidable mother; her baseball fandom.

There is that tender palpating thing.

Today a leaf on the screen door betrayed itself a moth by a sudden light movement that registered in the animal brain as breathing. A winged creature, double-fanned, mimicking a ginkgo-ish leaf, the wormy body below anchoring itself to the screen, unmoving even when one inadvertently let the door slam.

A breathing leaf.

A moth mimicking.

A midrange-green fan with two charred spots, eyes not for seeing.

The world a world of imitation; of likening; of attention; symbiosis.

From another angle: predation.

● ● ● ●

She has no heirs. She has several epigones but their detail-laden lacquered ships for me don't float. She flares singular, exemplary, a diamond absolute the American East forged in a pressure chamber we have yet fully to excavate.

It is said that, for all her formality, Marianne Moore spoke exactly the same to everyone—child, adult, servant, CEO, baseball player, college president. She was a true democrat.

One very often finds that in a Moore poem every phrase is load-bearing. This is sound architecture, the weight brilliantly distributed.

Throughout the work, there is the hard and soft. One finds not so much metamorphoses as interpenetration, as the sea slices rock in "The Wave" or the scaly thing reveals itself also to be a soft vulnerable mass (in "The Pangolin"). If her contemporaries often turned to myth (*The Waste Land*, *Ulysses*), to a new mode of modern enchantment, Moore made it new via a reverse enchantment: unlike Orpheus, she does not make the stones sing but rather sings the stones:

> I sense your glory.
> For things that I desire and have not got:
> For things I have that I wish I had not,
> > You compensate me,
> > Stones.

("FLINTS, NOT FLOWERS")

Hear this refusal to swoon, this song of lack, this almost New Englandy logic of flinty compensation. This bald rhythmic reckoning with, dispossession of, "things." In such a poem, an early poem, it is as if Moore moves behind Eliot's idea of the "objective correlative"—the object adequate to emotion, to a complex of thought and feeling—to show us the process by which "flints" might become that object, selected over and against "flowers." For as Milton said, and Moore surely knew, "reason is but choosing."

Which in Moore's case often means negating: "Flints, Not Flowers."

"The Mind Is an Enchanting Thing." So goes the title of a much later poem. What could be a fey little announcement—

how *enchanting* the mind!—is in Moore a diagnosis: the mind *enchants*: it casts spells, sings songs, projects its magic on and through the object world and other creatures. The poems tack between a submission to and a critique of this enchantment. They are anti-Orphic more than Orphic—yet one has to know the power of Orpheus to create a poetics opposed to it.

She does not make the animals speak; she speaks to the animal, *speaks to* in the sense of speaking toward the case.

● ● ● ●

Moore's famous impersonality is not the strenuous seductive pseudododge of Eliot's masks but the impersonality of perilously achieved *distance*. I will look at that *from here*. And now, *from here*. There is a scrupulous respecting of borders, of "boundaries," to invoke the current pop-psychological lexicon; in order to respect these edges one has to know where they might be—one has to move up to and alongside them, delicately. One has to feel out the parts of it all.

There is a great tact.

Some find it fussiness.

Tact: etymologically *touch*. Con-tact. The poems are astonishingly tactile, as in "The Pangolin"—

Another armored animal—scale
　　lapping scale with spruce-cone regularity until they
form the uninterrupted central
　tail-row! This near artichoke with head and legs and grit-
equipped gizzard
. . . .
. . . this ant- and stone-swallowing uninjurable
　　artichoke . . .

Uninjurable artichoke!
"O to be a dragon"!
"Armor seems extra" ("The Pangolin"), but it's not.
For: "but what about the predatory hand?" ("Roses Only")

● ● ● ●

It is instructive to consider H.D.'s "Sea Rose" alongside Marianne Moore's "Roses Only." H.D.'s poem, the first in her book *Sea Garden* (1916), in its entirety:

　　　　Rose, harsh rose,
　　　　marred and with stint of petals,
　　　　meagre flower, thin
　　　　sparse of leaf,

　　　　more precious
　　　　than a wet rose
　　　　single on a stem—
　　　　you are caught in the drift.

Stunted, with small leaf,
you are flung on the sand,
you are lifted
in the crisp sand
that drives in the wind.

Can the spice-rose
drip such acrid fragrance
hardened in a leaf?

Here we have the characteristic tones and gestures of the early H.D., the remarkable invocative power, the vaguely narcotized haze as the apostrophized flower is flung on the sand.

Here we have not the red red rose of age-old song, not Burns's beloved rose-likened, but something differently, intimately, addressed: *Rose, harsh rose*. Helplessly feminized, the rose stands in English lyric as the most overburdened of flowers, always already written but ready to be rewritten, reimagined as the "harsh rose," the "stunted" rose, the "marred" rose, the "sparse" rose and not (for example) Burns's fresh flower "newly sprung in June."

For as William Carlos Williams wrote, "The rose is obsolete." "But if it ends / the start is begun" (*Spring and All*).

H.D. gives us a sea rose marking not a season—of spring, of love, of blooming immanence, of sexuality vital or vulnerable—but rather an ontological susceptibility to the elements themselves: this rose "caught in the drift," flung by wavedrift or winddrift to the sand, itself a mobile harsh-grained element lifting the rose.

The rose transfigured, interrogated, transvalued:

> Can the spice-rose
> drip such acrid fragrance
> hardened in a leaf?

There is a languid, lethal, acrid sexuality here, a liminal edge-state pondered . . .

One notes the preponderance of monosyllables, the fatal heaviness of the lyric tread below its languorous drift, the peculiar genitives, as if this were a translation from a language simultaneously more formal and more immediate than English: this rose "marred and with stint of petals," "sparse of leaf," "with small leaf." One hears the sonorous repetitions of sound, the harsh clustering *st*: of *st*int, *st*unted playing against the several open *o*'s; the snaky sibilants of rose, precious, single on a stem, spice-rose; the swift short *i* of crisp and lifted and drift and wind, as if the *ih* sound drifted through the poem like the rose itself. One hears too the crescendo in the recapitulations of syntax: you are caught, you are flung, you are lifted—a progression of possession and transport, of being driven "on the sand," "in the wind."

●

After this intense enunciation, so freighted with lyric history, so mythopoeic in its elemental progressions, it is astonishing to turn to Moore's "Roses Only":

> You do not seem to realize that beauty is a liability rather
> > than
> an asset—that in view of the fact that spirit creates form
> > we are justified in supposing
> that you must have brains. . . .

Moore's discursive, intricately intellected address; its encompassing, technical, Latinate diction; its conceit of a legalistic, economistic calculus (liabilities and assets); its rapid modulations and syntactical complexities revealing a supremely ironic yet sensitive intelligence: all bear down on the rose, that fated emblem of the feminine.

"Roses Only" might be called "Against Roses Only." Its argument proposes that "You would look, minus / thorns—like a what-is-this, a mere / peculiarity." It is thorns, that is, that make for the rose's brilliance and singularity, for the roseness of the rose:

> Guarding the
> infinitesimal pieces of your mind, compelling audience to

the remark that it is better to be forgotten than to be
    remembered too violently,
  your thorns are the best part of you.

The rose's thorns align themselves with the pangolin's armor, the defensive element which marks the essence of the creature.

Not the sick rose (Blake) nor the flung rose but the thorned rose.

"Sea Rose" versus "Roses Only": H.D. versus Marianne Moore:

Incantation versus argument; lyric versus discourse; a strongly Anglo-Saxon lexical core versus a flagrantly Latinate repertoire. The vatic inward versus the detailed observed. The hieratic versus the potentially conversable. The presented versus the argued. The immanent versus the unfolded and deferred. The metaphoric versus the metonymic. The whole versus the part: "your thorns are the best part of you," you with your "infinitesimal pieces of . . . mind." The organic image versus the anatomized *topos*. The Romantic versus the Augustan. The sung versus the said. The felt versus the thought.

So it would seem.

It was and is to me very moving to see these two poets in the early twentieth century, so gifted, admiring of each other, moving differently yet perhaps rotating around a similar axis, the axis of that given rose, our given bodies, given languages. To see them both making it new, and making it new differently. To see the different powers they had and the forms and rhythms they found.

Roses and thorns and seas and sand and edges of the new, the ridges of the old.

"The rose is obsolete / but each petal ends in / an edge" (William Carlos Williams).

● ● ● ●

In the modern turn, return, to Adamic essentials, Moore stands alongside (albeit more decorously) D. H. Lawrence, with his own gardens, slithering snakes, raw sex, pulsing orifices, root-lust. In "Marriage," a poem reanimating Adam and Eve and their efforts of union, one watches her performance of scrupulously suspended judgment—though one feels, perhaps, knowing the gender of the poet, the special pathos of Eve's position. Yet Moore is as much an Adam as an Eve. Moore stations herself—

IN THE DAYS OF PRISMATIC COLOR

not in the days of Adam and Eve, but when Adam
    was alone; when there was no smoke and color was
fine, not with the refinement
    of early civilization art, but because
of its originality; with nothing to modify it but the

mist that went up . . .

This troping toward origins is always belated, always shad-
owed by a later knowledge, filtered through the discriminat-
ing mind: *not* in the days of Adam and Eve, *but*; *not* with the
refinement . . . *but*. We are in the days before division into gen-
der, before sex, before mingling, before modification: in the
pure serene of uncomplicated "originality." As if one could get
to the pure lyric site, before story, before declension in every
sense. When "obliqueness was a variation / of the perpendicu-
lar." As if one could be stationed in the world of appearance,
when appearance was essence and the world a world of pure
noun: when every man was the only man, Adam, his name his
kind; when every noun existed in only one case, undeclined.

Moore is a great namer and it is no accident that Adam stands
as her original poet, the place from which all declining—into
complexity, into obscurity—will be measured. Moore writes a
brilliantly sophisticated poetry with a direct connection to the

naive: the artist whose work is infamously complex, a poet who strikingly outflanks paraphrase, is also critical of false complexities:

> . . . complexity is not a crime, but carry
> it to the point of murkiness
>   and nothing is plain. Complexity,
> moreover, that has been committed to darkness, instead of
>
> granting itself to be the pestilence that it is, moves all a-
>   bout as if to bewilder us with the dismal
> fallacy that insistence
>   is the measure of achievement and that all
> truth must be dark. Principally throat, sophistication is as it al-
>
> ways has been—at the antipodes from the init-
>   ial great truths.

("IN THE DAYS OF PRISMATIC COLOR")

Moore's peculiar power often arises from this complicated dance between apparent statement and specific means— between, say, this critique of complexity and her syntactically complex enactment of it; between her dismissal of mere formalism and a triumph of invented form, the network of rhymes and patterned syllabics:

> . . . Truth is no Apollo
> Belvedere, no formal thing. The wave may go over it if it likes.

Know that it will be there when it says,
"I shall be there when the wave has gone by."

("IN THE DAYS OF PRISMATIC COLOR")

This knotty conclusion reworks, among many precedents, Keats's famously resolved antimony between Truth and Beauty in his "Ode on a Grecian Urn": " 'Beauty is truth, truth beauty,'—that is all / Ye know on earth, and all ye need to know."

In Keats we have a speaking urn, with its chiasmic emblem, the famously asserted equation

$$Truth = Beauty \, / \, Beauty = Truth$$

which readers and critics have pondered and picked at since.

What do we need to know?

Know that it will be there when it says,
"I shall be there when the wave has gone by."

The "formal thing," the "Apollo Belvedere" of civilization, submits to the wave, which may do what it likes. Truth will (still) be there when the wave has gone by.

Something imperishable persists, something that "is no formal thing" but which may yet be embodied in the Apollo Belvedere—an Ursprung of making that exceeds any particular made thing. There is a riddling undoing in these lines that accounts, in part, for their haunting. Antecedents wobble in the wave:

The wave may go over it if it likes.

May go over what: Truth? The Apollo Belvedere? And by extension any "formal thing"?

Know that it will be there when it says:

What will be there: Truth? The Apollo Belvedere?

"I shall be there when the wave goes by."

Who or what speaks this final line?

I had thought Truth. But it may be the Apollo Belvedere itself speaking the last line, persisting though shattered in the wave, still speaking to the case of what persists even if chiseled form and unity are smashed.

• • • •

Moore shows the beauty and the poverty of information. Her poems are *informed*, formed by that which is in them. In Moore a fact becomes a "luminous detail" (à la Pound) but also retains some of the aura of its discursive origin: as a scientific fact, a historical fact, a physiological fact, a geological fact, a journalistic fact—data for stitching, or (to shift metaphors) for inlaying into the irregular yet measured mosaic of the poem.

There is a risk in fetishizing the wrought quality of Moore's poems, a risk in using such analogies as "mosaic," since this suggests an inanimate, decorative thing. And some find Moore's poems thus. Yet her poems shuttle between the hammered gold and gold enameling of artifice and the messy breathing dripping creaturely life she also attends to:

> . . . In the short-legged, fit-
> ful advance, the gurgling and all the minutiae—we have the
> classic

multitude of feet.

("IN THE DAYS OF PRISMATIC COLOR")

The gurgling as well as the minutiae, the subarticulate creaturely babble as well as the "classic" hardness of a wrought urn or a thrown pot. She gives us a caterpillared mind, with a multitude of living feet as well as metrical feet. Her sense of the multiplicity of things, and the interpenetrability of matter and idea, soft and hard, high and low, creates that special tacking through the ocean of sentience that is her forte. For truly she sees us as (like the butterfly):

HALF DEITY

half worm.

For all the perfected things in her poems, the perfected things that are her poems, there is also lurking, surging, creeping—

> the raw material of poetry in
> all its rawness
>
> **("POETRY")**

Yes she is far more Cooked than Raw, but let's throw the lady a bone.

As she was brought to animals, sculptures, glass figurines, to complex made things, so too we are brought to metaphors of making when exploring the peculiar *poiesis* of Moore's work.

> *To explain grace requires / a curious hand.*
>
> **("THE PANGOLIN")**

Williams defined the poem as a small, or large, machine made of words. Moore's poems may be the best exemplum of Williams's dictum; instead of devolving into the merely mechanical, they are wonderful contraptions (in the full sense of wonder) that at their best breathe a sentient life.

> . . . A sailboat
>
> was the first machine. Pangolins, made
> for moving quietly also, are models of exactness . . .

The thing itself, and the idea about the thing: the pangolin in its scaled specificity, and the pangolin, the "model of exactness," "moving quietly."

• • • •

At her worst, she is twee, or, alternately, insistent. She could seem prudish, famously advising Elizabeth Bishop to delete "watercloset" from her poem "Roosters." One could not imagine her liking, much less writing like, Sharon Olds. But perhaps this is unfair to both poets: there is more bodily mess and more extreme emotion in Moore than one might think. Moore is ill-served by many of her admirers, who put her on the mantel with Aunt Jennifer's tigers, precious and breakable and old-fashioned, or who see her as a specimen of lovable eccentric poetic Americana. Americans like their artists folksy, palsy, just plain folks writing plain poems *in plain American which cats and dogs can read!* ("England"). She ran the risk of becoming a character and the weaker poems may suffer from that.

But she is the stealth weapon of American poetry, with a ferocity and a lacerating intelligence few poets have matched. She has a capacity for a Swiftian savage indignation, and for a courtly feline bitchiness one finds more regularly in Saint-Simon and Proust. Her very titles can be amusing little cracks of the whip: "In This Age of Hard Trying, Nonchalance Is Good and." "To Be Liked by You Would Be a Calamity." Like Pound, who wrote extremely funny character sketches and savage epigrams, she occasionally offers mordant little epitaphs on encounters with inflated morons and presumptuous numbskulls:

> I am hard to disgust,
>> but a pretentious poet can do it;
>> a person without a tap root; and
>> impercipience can do it; did it.
>>> ("MERCIFULLY")

Her pointed social satires remind one of Jane Austen, her baroque syntactical devastations reminiscent of Henry James:

I remember a swan under the willows in Oxford,
    with flamingo-colored, maple-
        leaflike feet. It reconnoitered like a battle-
ship. Disbelief and conscious fastidiousness were
    ingredients in its
        disinclination to move. Finally its hardihood was
            not proof against its
        proclivity to more fully appraise such bits
            of food as the stream

bore counter to it; it made away with what I gave it
    to eat. I have seen this swan and

> I have seen you; I have seen ambition without
> understanding in a variety of forms.
>
> ("CRITICS AND CONNOISSEURS")

At how many inane social gatherings, or when watching how many porcine politicians on TV, might one take solace in these exhilarating lines!

> *I have seen this swan and*
> *I have seen you.*
>
> *I have seen ambition without*
> *understanding in a variety of forms.*

The ostentatious Latinate polysyllables (disinclination, proclivity), the intricate clauses, all move toward the punch of the monosyllabic epitaph: *I have seen this swan and I have seen you.* The thing itself, an observed scene, then glossed: *I have seen ambition without understanding in a variety of forms.* The emblem, the image, the gloss: the medieval emblem book made modern. Her epigrammatic wit is simultaneously a spine straightener and a consolation. There should be a Marianne Moore brand of bourbon. "Neatness of finish! Neatness of finish!" ("The Octopus"). She was unafraid to be intelligent, to know what she knew, to question what she knew, to learn new things, to sit in uncertainties (Keats) for all her infamous "capacity for fact," her "relentless accuracy" ("The Octopus"), and her aura of positivity. A poetry of knowledge but not a knowing poetry: an ongoing beacon.

•

One finds in Moore a whiplashing capacity for self-critique, the poems remaking their premises across as well as within works—one poem concluding with a salute to "that weapon, self-protectiveness":

> The staff, the bag, the feigned inconsequence
> of manner, best bespeak that weapon, self-protectiveness.
> ("IN THIS AGE OF HARD TRYING, NONCHALANCE IS GOOD AND")

another poem diagnosing the rigidity thereof:

> What is
>   there in being able
>   to say that one has dominated the stream in an attitude
>   of self-defense,
>   in proving that one has had the experience
>   of carrying a stick?
>   ("CRITICS AND CONNOISSEURS")

To paraphrase what Emerson said of Thoreau, she felt herself best in opposition. Perhaps this is why it was she who wrote a most brilliant anatomy of modern marriage, in "Marriage"—

> One sees that it is rare—
> that striking grasp of opposites
> opposed each to the other, not to unity.

• • • •

It is remarkable that one of the best poems of the twentieth century, Moore's "Marriage," is apparently so little read. The best poem on marriage since, perhaps, *Paradise Lost*, to which it is enormously and confidently indebted. A poem on the romance, the fatality, of marriage, by a woman whom some could not but see as *a spinster*.

They toil not, neither do they spin.

But toil she did, and spin, a queer erotic weave suffused with feeling; an American original Pound and Williams had the great fortune and insight to hail.

As Williams said of Emily Dickinson and might have said of Moore: *She was a real good guy*.

Opposition is true friendship, said Blake.

But this is not about friendship—this is about marriage:

> This institution,
> perhaps one should say enterprise
> out of respect for which
> one says one need not change one's mind

> about a thing one has believed in,
> requiring public promises
> of one's intention
> to fulfill a private obligation:
> I wonder what Adam and Eve
> think of it by this time . . .

One hears here a new note, not exactly a new tone—though a new tone sounds within this long, moving, weird, and grief-struck poem—but a new pace, an enormously *caretaking* pace, a slow regular walking step, as we move phrase by thinking phrase down the line, down the page.

It is perhaps obvious that we are talking here, that Moore was talking here, of heterosexual marriage. About that state-sponsored "institution" or "perhaps one should say enterprise" organizing what Adrienne Rich later called "the tragedy of sex." Meaning, at the time she wrote, the tragedy of hetero sex.

Though this tragedy need not be confined to any locality or mode of sex.

The voice: a polemically neutral or rather clinical speaker, deploying an ostentatiously impersonal pronoun: perhaps *one* should say enterprise; perhaps *one* need not change *one's* mind.

"Marriage" is in part a poem about seeing whether one need change one's mind.
This presumes that women have minds—
which has long been doubtful
—even if occasionally "we are justified in supposing / that you must have brains" ("Roses Only").

Need one "change one's mind / about a thing one has believed in"? Are these carefully unfolding phrases a concession to all those who continue to regard marriage as "a thing one has believed in," the opening clauses offered "out of respect" to those who continue to believe by one who might not?

We are in the presence of a dramatized scrupulosity as the poet *considers the case.* It is, then, with extreme precision that Moore gives us a strenuously ungendered, apparently unmarked speaker: ONE. It is as if she stands outside or beyond gender and indeed beyond the species, or rather that she aims for that position, that generous godlike yet unsexed position from which to assess them both, gently mocking, shaking the head. She forces us to reckon with the position of the speaker, generalized and impersonal as that *one*, but also, equally, forced into that impersonality, as if too close to a very live wire—

I wonder what Adam and Eve / think of it by this time.

•

Apparently unmarked, this *one* has adopted a rhetorical distance: her seemingly neutral *one* is in fact marked—for "experience attests / that men have power / and sometimes one is made to feel it."

A poem about the possibility, the impossibility, of two-becoming-one, about a He and a She becoming, perhaps, a We, about a You and an I becoming an US: Moore reckons with marriage—and reckons throughout "Marriage"—in the most essential, that is to say grammatical, terms.

Before the noun: the pronoun.
He.
She.
One.

• • • •

Moore gives us the elemental thing, a man and a woman, a garden, a snake—"that invaluable accident / exonerating Adam." She gives us too the historical thing, that brazen New Woman stalking the cultural imaginary (and the shops and offices and city streets) of the 1920s, with her sexual knowledge, her urban sophistication, her cheap information-stuffed *nowness*:

> I have seen her
> when she was so handsome
> she gave me a start,
> able to write simultaneously
> in three languages—
> English, German, and French—
> and talk in the meantime ...

The poem is simultaneously a celebration of opposition-in-marriage and a requiem for the possibility of its ever actually flourishing:

> this amalgamation which can never be more
> than an interesting impossibility ...

This is a poem passionately inquiring into what theorists might call "the sex/gender system of companionate marriage"—a poem asking whether egalitarian marriage might work, and how: questions that, centuries before, were Milton's as well.

Moore approaches the *topos* gingerly, carefully, judiciously and mock-judiciously, as if committed to laying out all aspects of the case. She offers a forensic essay—an assay, an attempt, a testing; it is a sifting of evidence, drawn from a vast cultural inheritance here mobilized with a sorrowing wit.

•

She writes for the defense and for the prosecution, in a sustained performance of due diligence:

> Eve: beautiful woman—
> I have seen her
> when she was so handsome
> she gave me a start . . .
> . . . .
> "See her, see her in this common world,"
> the central flaw
> in that first crystal-fine experiment . . .

And of Adam:

> And he has beauty also;
> it's distressing—the O thou
> to whom from whom,
> without whom nothing—Adam . . .

Partisanship withers in the distress of this witnessing, this recognition of this double beauty. And it is as if the poet cannot see Adam without invoking Eve's own response to Adam, as Milton imagined it in *Paradise Lost*. There Eve's address moves immediately into the syntax of dependency and of idolatry:

> . . . O thou for whom
> and from whom I was formed, flesh of thy flesh,
> and without whom am to no end . . .
>
> (*PARADISE LOST*, BOOK IV)

Adam is her pre-position: made from his rib, she is of him, from him, for him, without him nothing. Her relation to God is always already mediated—*He for God only, she for God in him* (*Paradise Lost*, Book IV).

In Moore, Eve's Miltonic salutation becomes a kind of semi-ironized, fatal shorthand, with Adam glossed as "the O thou / to whom from whom, without whom nothing—Adam": an apposition semi-ironized in the poet's handling, because one must concede that "he has beauty also," that he should be adored; because one feels—

> the strange experience of beauty;
> its existence is too much;
> it tears one to pieces
> and each fresh wave of consciousness
> is poison.

This staggers me always, the abrupt shifts of tone, the movement from the forensic to this sudden impassioned lyric outbreak that does not exalt but rather sears. After all the mock-heroic presentation of our first parents, after this apparent distancing from them--

> What can one do for them—
> these savages

Amid all the argufying the poem enacts, we are suddenly plunged into a remembered world of prelapsarian lyric, a song of impossibility—

> Below the incandescent stars
> below the incandescent fruit,
> the strange experience of beauty;
> its existence is too much;
> it tears one to pieces
> and each fresh wave of consciousness
> is poison.

Yeats said that out of the argument with others, one makes rhetoric; out of the argument with oneself, poetry. "Marriage" is a higher-order *poiesis*, a sustained argument with oneself conducted through the medium of rhetoric. Within the poem it is Adam who makes the case for marriage, in a stately, slightly pompous formal rhetoric that ingathers phrasing and diction from a myriad of sources as we hear him—

> commending it
> as a fine art, as an experiment,
> a duty or as merely recreation.
> One must not call him ruffian
> nor friction a calamity—
> the fight to be affectionate:
> "no truth can be fully known
> until it has been tried
> by the tooth of disputation."

While

> She says, "This butterfly,
> this waterfly, this nomad
> that has 'proposed
> to settle on my hand for life'—
> What can one do with it?"

A glorious "he says, she says" exchange unfolds, as if Moore were staging her own George Cukor comedy.

Moore gives us two beautiful subjects speaking past each other. As Freud knew, as Lacan knew, as one is given by life to know: one speaks past as well as to the other. I is another; one speaks past oneself. Where I am, it shall be.

Here we have one subject speaking more, this Adam "alive with words," fatally committed to the power of speech, dedicated to persuasion, inflamed with visions of progress—

> Alive with words,
> vibrating like a cymbal
> touched before it has been struck,
> he has prophesied correctly—
> the industrious waterfall,
> "the speedy stream
> which violently bears all before it,
> at one time silent as the air
> and now powerful as the wind."

The poem both satirizes and honors male heroism. And it rings many changes on age-old misogynistic themes, offering its own catalog of details; there is of course a powerful male case against marriage and Moore is keen to present it: "The fact of woman / is 'not the sound of the flute' / but very poison." In a polyphonic, polemical orchestration of quoted bits, Moore brilliantly adopts and parries the voice of one who asserts—

> ". . . 'a wife is a coffin,'
> that severe object
> with the pleasing geometry
> stipulating space not people,
> refusing to be buried
> and uniquely disappointing,
> revengefully wrought in the attitude
> of an adoring child
> to a distinguished parent."

That it was Ezra Pound who spoke the wife-is-a-coffin line opens up new angles. Such an exchange between the He and the She could be endless, has been endless, and Moore will give no obvious resolution. She offers instead a kind of diagnosis.

There is a terminal, foundational, incorrigible *mistaking*—of the self, of the other:

The fact forgot
that "some have merely rights
while some have obligations,"
he loves himself so much,
he can permit himself
no rival in that love.
She loves herself so much,
she cannot see herself enough—
a statuette of ivory on ivory,
the logical last touch
to an expansive splendor
earned as wages for work done . . .

The whole poem partakes of the rhetoric of the *dubitatio*:

Psychology which explains everything
explains nothing,
and we are still in doubt.

and of an impossibility trope tested and retested—

this amalgamation which can never be more
than an interesting impossibility . . .

Yet—

One sees that it is rare—
that striking grasp of opposites
opposed each to the other, not to unity . . .

One sees that it is rare; rare, that is, but perhaps possible.

• • • •

In her final lines, Moore moves us from

> . . . that experiment of Adam's
> with ways out but no way in—
> the ritual of marriage . . .

into another experiment in Union:

> "Liberty and Union
> now and forever" . . .

the marriage plight tellingly phrased—rephrased, quoted—in terms from Daniel Webster's famous speech arguing against the proposed doctrine of nullification: Webster's Second Reply to Hayne, of January 26, 1830. Webster, the great Democratic orator of and for the Union, he who watched it crumble. We end with "the essence of the matter"—that "experiment of Adam's"—decisively transformed into a political question as well as an ethical, erotic, aesthetic question. A meditation on "this institution" becomes a reflection on "constitution." We end with an image of Daniel Webster, sculpted, historical, "the Book on the writing table; / The hand on the breast-pocket." We might recall that Webster argued against nullification, the doctrine that a state could refuse to obey a federal law. Moore has been conducting her own experiment in nullification, all the while paying her deep-felt dues to the promise of—

"Liberty and Union
now and forever" . . .

One may hear in this a pointed silence as well: Webster's fa-
mous phrases typically ring out in memory thus: *Liberty and
Union, Now and Forever, One and Inseparable.*

Moore does not include Webster's "One and Inseparable."
Its existence is too much; it tears one to pieces.

● ● ● ●

I first read Moore seriously when I was studying at Oxford; I
had also been reading in various schools of feminism and psy-
choanalysis, as they were in the air in those days, and as I
needed tools for living. Moore's poem may have taught me
more than any debate between Anglo-American and French
feminists, or between, say, object-relations and Lacanian an-
alysts. Or perhaps it taught me nothing; poems aren't for
teaching; they insinuate; they are of the Tree of Life and of the
Tree of Knowledge; they are "something feline, / something
colubrine." As wizards of projection, anthropomorphism and
trope, poets have their own long history of singing the song
of *introjection*, of *transference*, of *projection*. And of course, of
meditating on Woman.

●

Woman as ideal, as bane, as muse, as mother, as lover, as daughter, as harpy, shrew, whore, and bliss.
Woman under erasure.

> She loves herself so much,
> she cannot see herself enough—

Female narcissism. The feminine as narcissism. Woman as lack.

What sentient woman does not know all about this, does not live this out? What man does not also, in another way, live this out?

The horrible endless iteration of it all. The Dark Continent of It All endlessly explored.

What do women want?

> "*I* should like to be alone";
> to which the visitor replies,
> "I should like to be alone;
> why not be alone together?"

Woman as a mess of contradictions, as She Who Does Not Know Her Own Mind: viz. Moore's Eve,

> equally positive in demanding a commotion
> and in stipulating quiet:

And it is true I did not know my own mind.

I wrote a long essay comparing Moore's poetics with H.D.'s and Gertrude Stein's; I read them intensively; I got engaged to be married; I thought and felt and felt and thought and floated ever more perilously away from myself, for I needed a kind of saving no one would offer and I could not provide myself. I read myself into all the contradictions; I knew the bourgeois bankruptcy of marriage, the long eviscerating history of it, the pleasures that might be found within it; I was engaged to a man who was kind and intelligent and loving and seemingly open to every thought, however disturbing. He was unfazed by con-tradiction, a maven of poststructuralist thinking, a person who tended to approach literature as a game for amused de-coding. Print is dead, he would say cheerfully. Anything you write is fine with me, he would say, a great gift to one unsanc-tioned by family or background to write. I thought ours were equal and opposite searchings, but I had my own violent promptings and urgencies which he did not, could not, share, and the compulsion or impulsion to pursue these promptings was itself a weird eros that further drove me on, off—

I had fallen in love with another but not it would seem out of love with him. This was unwieldy. This was worse: It was a contradiction, a flaw in the world, unencompassable, "the central flaw / in that first crystal-fine experiment," and every-thing shattered.

•

For I was in fact out of love with him but not with the globe that had seemingly enclosed us. And the woman I now loved was a darting thing, flickering and uncapturable, given to pronouncements like, *Well, that is what one does, no? Marry. Everyone of course feels ambivalent.*

This was to me outrageous as well as a great grief.
My great vocation was *not to feel ambivalent*.
This was, of course, childish. It bespoke the vain purity of the child.
Which I should have honored.

> . . . satisfaction is a lowly
> thing, how pure a thing is joy.
> **("WHAT ARE YEARS")**

For our wedding ceremony I chose passages to be read during the liturgy. It was to be a Catholic mass—every element of the experience becoming a thorough immolation of the self on the bier of given expectation. The wedding dress—one my parents preferred; the mass, residual ritual of my upbringing; the marriage itself, a public consecration of the right to be an adult, that is to have sex, and to answer to no one except those to whom one chose to answer.

•

This bespoke a peculiarly impoverished sense of adulthood.
Liberty and Union, now and forever.
This was a form of self-directed soul-murder. As well as,
more obviously, a revolting abuse of my soon-to-be husband.

> What can one do for them—
> these savages

There was nothing to be done or nothing I could do and no one
could or did help me, nor did anyone help him. I chose a poem
for the liturgy that I thought might honor and see us through
this difficulty—

> The ache of marriage:
>
> thigh and tongue, beloved,
> are heavy with it,
> it throbs in the teeth
>
> We look for communion
> and are turned away, beloved,
> each and each
>
> It is leviathan and we
> in its belly
> looking for joy, some joy
> not to be known outside it

two by two in the ark of
the ache of it.

(DENISE LEVERTOV,
"THE ACHE OF MARRIAGE")

We were in the ark of it, the ache of it, though our aches were different and the ark of our covenant ultimately, necessarily, belatedly broken.

this amalgamation which can never be more
than an interesting impossibility . . .

became an excruciating impossibility. Below the incandescent stars, below the incandescent fruit, something was broken and there was nothing to be done and

it tears one to pieces
and each fresh wave of consciousness
is poison.

When but to think was to be full of sorrow, when to be conscious was to wish to be dead, when in some moods one had to admit—

"I am such a cow,
if I had a sorrow
I should feel it a long time;

I am not one of those
who have a great sorrow
in the morning
and a great joy at noon . . ."

—there was this other prior thing of thinking sorrow, this
wonderful keening and sometimes ludic thing. In the midst of
all rending and beyond all unknowing there is a gratitude for
those who survey what's impossible, for those who say that
"love / is the only fortress / strong enough to trust to" ("Paper
Nautilus"), those who cry out saying—

. . . If that which is at all were not forever,
why would those who graced the spires
with animals and gathered there to rest, on cold luxurious
low stone seats—a monk and monk and monk—between the thus
    ingenious roof-supports, have slaved to confuse
        grace with a kindly manner, time in which to pay a debt,
    the cure for sins, a graceful use
of what are yet
        approved stone mullions branching out across
        the perpendiculars? . . .

("THE PANGOLIN")

a gratitude for those who wonder *if that which is at all were not
forever*, how to persist—

What is our innocence,
what is our guilt? All are
naked, none is safe. . . .

("WHAT ARE YEARS")

All honor to those who wave the pure flag of a difficult joy—

So he who strongly feels,
behaves. The very bird,
grown taller as he sings, steels
his form straight up. Though he is captive,
his mighty singing
says, satisfaction is a lowly
thing, how pure a thing is joy.
This is mortality,
this is eternity.

("WHAT ARE YEARS")

8.

MY H.D.

The anonymous collective wisdom of Wikipedia will tell you that H.D. is "an American poet, novelist and memoirist known for her association with the early 20th century avant-garde Imagist group of poets such as Ezra Pound and Richard Aldington." She retains the aura of a Delphic priestess, a queer cultic charisma that appealed to waves of self-selected members of the elect—in the early years Ezra Pound, William Carlos Williams, Richard Aldington (her first husband), D. H. Lawrence; later such attendants as Norman Holmes Pearson; and still later, after her death, other scholars, often feminist, who brought her life and work back into focus in the 1970s and 1980s. And there is too an ongoing esoteric line of influence—transference? discipleship? inhabitation? telepathy?—that continues through poets' transmissions and study, Robert Duncan's *H.D. Book* and, in another key, Barbara Guest's *Herself Defined* among the notable monuments of this line.

•

"Little, but all roses." What the ancient poet Meleager said of Sappho, of the broken fragmentary inheritance she'd left. What H.D. echoes in *The Wise Sappho* (1919): "Little but all roses!" Confronted with 612 pages of poetry in the New Directions edition of *H.D.: Collected Poems, 1912–1944*, one might say, "Much, and only some roses."

For surely as she was undervalued at various junctures of the past century, she has also been in some quarters indiscriminately praised. Out of some six hundred pages perhaps some fifty are dear to me; though I would recommend to anyone her World War II epic *Trilogy*, and reserve a special fondness for *Helen in Egypt*, a late work that restages in a Greek key aspects of her analysis with Freud, Theseus here playing the psychopomp to an unjustly reviled Helen.

While the later, longer, more discursive, mythico-narrative works are a certain achievement, and important documents of twentieth-century war writing and of the long poem, I am marking here what most marked me.

It is no dispraise to be a poet best served by an anthology, a rigorously pruned selected—no dispraise particularly for this poet, who knew very well that "anthology" comes from the Greek: a gathering of flowers. "Little, but all roses."

•

Some roses—from her first book *Sea Garden* (1916):

> Rose, harsh rose,
>
> marred and with stint of petals,
>
> meagre flower, thin...
>
> ("SEA ROSE")

> You are clear
>
> O rose, cut in rock,
>
> hard as the descent of hail.
>
> ("GARDEN")

and also poppies:

> Amber husk
>
> fluted with gold,
>
> fruit on the sand
>
> marked with a rich grain...
>
> ("SEA POPPIES")

These early lyrics show one aspect of her characteristic best—
they bespeak "H.D., Imagiste," baptized thus by Pound, in a fa-
mous meeting in the tearoom of the British Museum in 1912.
He had the manifesto-ing impulse, the impresario's gift, and
here—along with some few of his own poems, and Aldington's,
and eventually a few others'—here he found his exempla: here
were poems sloughing off the slithering excesses of Georgian
verse, the adjectival fripperies, the Latinate involutions, the

flight from precision. Here, as in "Hermes of the Ways"—the poem that prompted Pound's christening "H.D., Imagiste" and appeared in Harriet Monroe's *Poetry* in 1913—one finds a version of what Pound called for, "An 'Image' . . . which presents an intellectual and emotional complex in an instant of time" ("A Retrospect"). One finds a validation of his dicta:

1. Direct treatment of the "thing" whether subjective or objective.
2. To use absolutely no word that does not contribute to the presentation.
3. As regarding rhythm: to compose in the sequence of the musical phrase, not in the sequence of a metronome.

But H.D.'s poems, like Pound's "In a Station of the Metro," were never only exempla.

• • • •

H.D. was extremely good, especially as a young poet, at generating objective correlatives for complex emotional states. Or rather, for a narrow band of emotional states—intense suspension, passionate rejection, inflamed supplication, ravaged and ravaging ambivalence, despondence, and, occasionally, ecstasy. Her first book, *Sea Garden*, is filled with successes in this line, her sea roses, sea lilies, and sea poppies all incarnating a complicated, paradoxically fierce delicacy, a kind of triumphant shattering, rent perfection—

> Reed,
> slashed and torn
> . . . .
> . . . you are shattered
> in the wind.
> . . . .
> Yet though the whole wind
> slash at your bark,
> you are lifted up . . .
> ("SEA LILY")

> O wind, rend open the heat,
> cut apart the heat,
> rend it to tatters.
> ("GARDEN")

Her diction, her phrasing, her repertoire of images is willfully constricted, as if she had confined herself to one or two modes, Lydian, say, or Doric, sounding each tone and interval on a single-stringed instrument—

> Can the spice-rose
> drip such acrid fragrance
> hardened in a leaf?
>
> ("SEA ROSE")

Her gardens are violently agitated border zones, austere, wind-torn, and sea-lashed; they are not the *hortus conclusus* of Eden or pastoral, nor the scented gardens of Arabia or Jerusalem, nor the bowers of bliss of Italy transported to England.

> honey is not more sweet
> than the salt stretch of your beach.
>
> ("THE SHRINE")

Her Sea Garden is lit

> by a desperate sun
> that struggles through sea-mist.
>
> ("HERMES OF THE WAYS")

By temperament and experience she was attuned to the Greek conviction that love was as much affliction as blessing—

> *Eros . . . bittersweet.*

which Anne Carson has so brilliantly plumbed.

Because she is so strongly associated with a subset of *verse libre*, of early-twentieth-century Anglophone free verse, her

achievement as a rhymer and as a metrist is perhaps over-
looked—for once you tune in, you cannot but hear her subtle
yet obsessive rhyming,

> is song's gift best?
> is love's gift loveliest?

and you can't but hear the intricate play of *take, slake, break,
and wake* throughout her "Fragment Thirty-six," or the re-
sounding pyre of desire in "The Master"—

> I did not know how to differentiate
> between volcanic desire,
> anemones like embers
> and purple fire
> of violets

—as she weighs the volcanic "red heat" of her desire for one
love against the lure of the "cold / silver / of her feet";

and you cannot but hear in her well-judged repetitions, her
identical rhymes (the zero degree of rhyme), how earned are
these recurrences. They figure the intense, even obsessive
attentiveness that is the hallmark of her best work—

> what meadow yields
> so fragrant a leaf
> as your bright leaf?
>
> ("SEA POPPIES")

Here and elsewhere she deploys repetition as much to disso-ciate as to emphasize: the terms of comparison widen as the word "leaf" recurs, the meadow leaf decisively distinguished from the hymned *fragrant bright leaf* of the "Sea Poppies."

Nor can you not respond to her command of "intricate songs' lost measure" ("Epitaph"). Through her study of Greek she found a way to give the heave to the pentameter (to paraphrase Pound), to approximate without strain the varied "dart and pulse" of Greek measures so long obscured by other treads.

She learned from Sappho and from the Greek tragedians; in Sappho she found not only lines, measures, situations, inten-sities, a whole erotic repertoire and key, but a deep-structural orientation to erotic triangles that resonated with her own—thus Sappho:

> In my eyes he matches the gods, that man who
> sits there facing you—any man whatever—
> listening from closeby to the sweetness of your
> voice as you talk, the
>
> sweetness of your laughter . . .
> ("FRAGMENT 31," TRANS. JIM POWELL)

and—

> *Thou flittest to Andromeda—*

and thus H. D., bringing her bitter offering to Aphrodite—

> I offer you this:
> (grant only strength
> that I withdraw not my gift,)
> I give you my praise and this:
> the love of my lover
> for his mistress.
>
> ("FRAGMENT FORTY-ONE")

Through Sappho she explored as well a kind of somatic poetics, a kind of sensually incarnational NOW—
—which underlies the seizure, the transport, of Sappho's "Fragment 31," when the beloved's voice and appearance and laughter

> sets the heart to shaking inside my breast, since
> once I look at you for a moment, I can't
>   speak any longer,
>
> but my tongue breaks down, and then all at once a
> subtle fire races inside my skin, my
> eyes can't see a thing and a whirring whistle
>   thrums at my hearing,
>
> cold sweat covers me and a trembling takes
> ahold of me all over: I'm greener than the

grass is and appear to myself to be little
short of dying . . .

(TRANS. JIM POWELL)

—and underlies H.D.'s development of "Fragment Thirty-six":

I know not what to do:
strain upon strain,
sound surging upon sound
makes my brain blind . . .

—and underlies Sappho's "Fragment 47":

Eros shook my
mind like a mountain wind falling on oak trees

(TRANS. ANNE CARSON)

—and underlies H.D.'s:

that will be me
to send a shudder through you,
cold wind

through an aspen tree

("SIGIL")

For all her capacity for swoon there is also the tough slap, the
sharp turn, the riposte, the counterpunch, the hard swerve—

I could scrape the colour
from the petals
like spilt dye from a rock.

("GARDEN")

I envy you your chance of death,
how I envy you this.

("FRAGMENT SIXTY-EIGHT")

spare us the beauty
of fruit-trees.

("ORCHARD")

Amid the sculpted intensities, the sounded-out extremities,
we find too the salutary disgust with beauty, with the pretty,
the lovely, the merely ornamental. The taut early work is as-
cetic, purged.

O for some sharp swish of a branch—
there is no scent of resin
in this place,
no taste of bark, of coarse weeds,
aromatic, astringent—
only border on border of scented pinks.
. . . .
For this beauty,
beauty without strength,
chokes out life.

I want wind to break,

scatter these pink-stalks,

snap off their spiced heads,

fling them about with dead leaves . . .

("SHELTERED GARDEN")

Here is a poet whose narrow yet prodigious strengths run perilously close to her weaknesses. A poet of passionate intensity, she must rely on a perfect pitch. When there is strain in her work, she runs the risk of a false or willed swooning, a mandated abjection. Yet among the states she is so brilliant at evoking is the transfigured and transfiguring abjection of the lover. That this posture is all too familiar for women makes for some uncomfortable reading—not because women should not explore erotic abjection but because its rendering can become quite predictably banal. One can of course find many examples of a kindred overreaching and emphatic swooning in the work of male poets, viz. Shelley: "I fall upon the thorns of life! I bleed!" ("Ode to the West Wind"); "I pant, I sink, I tremble, I expire!" ("Epipsychidion"). And Keats is notoriously full of bathetic heroes and overgilded lilies. Here one walks on very interesting terrain, the terrain of mastery and power. For no real poet, no serious reader, does not respect mastery and power; the question is, what kind of mastery, what power?

● ● ● ●

Consider a poem whose vocation in print began in 1914, "Oread":

> Whirl up sea—
> whirl your pointed pines,
> splash your great pines
> on our rocks,
> hurl your green over us,
> cover us with your pools of fir.

An apparently slight poem but a world-brightening poem, a poem of immediate mythic authority and vocal power, H.D.'s Oread, her mountain nymph, here apostrophizes the sea, as so many of her human brethren have—that sea "cold dark deep and absolutely clear," as Elizabeth Bishop wrote, "element bearable to no mortal."

A long tradition holds that poetry is, if not thinking per se, close to, kindred to, thought: as Heidegger observed in "The Thinker as Poet" (1947), "Singing and thinking are the stems neighbor to poetry." And Hannah Arendt in her book *The Human Condition* specifically remarked the proximity of poetry to "the thought that inspired it": "Poetry, whose material is language, is perhaps the most human and least worldly of the arts, the one in which the end product remains closest to the thought that inspired it." And Arendt further observed, "Of all things of thought, poetry is closest to thought, and a poem is less a thing than any other work of art."

●

So a poem, "less a thing than any other work of art," is yet a "thing of thought." *Whirl up sea. Whirl your pointed pines. Splash your great pines on our rocks.* The lure of the barely yet decisively reified thing, the hardly rendered poetic "thing of thought," the only-just-artifactualized voice: this is one appeal of the Oread's call. Over the years I have found myself often drawn to poems that project themselves forth less as monument than as song or spell, less as artifact than as enunciation. Or rather I oscillate, fascinated, between what I think of as two poles marking the limits of a highly variegated poetic spectrum. H.D.'s "Oread" versus, or alongside, Yeats's "Sailing to Byzantium." Or James Schuyler's apparently casual watercolors against, or alongside, Frank Bidart's awesomely wrought "The Second Hour of the Night."

H.D.'s "Oread" has seemingly barely made it over the threshold of artifactualization though it is decisively enunciated. The poem bespeaks the logic of artifactualizing thought: the poem appears as if from an archaic world of ritual incantation, a fragment of our mythic inheritance, in which to speak was to command the elements.
Splash your great pines on our rocks. Cover us with your pools of fir.

●

Nietzsche suggested and Derrida after him that behind every thought, within every concept, lies a figure, a trope: "Abstract notions always conceal a sensible [sensory] figure," Derrida observed in the "Exergue" to *White Mythology*. Turning from philosophy to poetry, Paul de Man was happy to follow Nietzsche down this sublimely figurative road in his essay "Anthropomorphism and Trope in Lyric." More recently, in *Poetry and the Fate of the Senses*, Susan Stewart has illuminated the profoundly anthropomorphic wagers of lyric. Invoking Vico's account of "*poiesis* as a process of anthropomorphization," she writes, "Vico explains that the imagination stems from bodily or 'corporeal senses' and is moved to represent itself by anthropomorphizing nature and by giving being to inanimate things." Stewart further suggests that "only when poetic metaphors make available to others the experience of the corporeal senses can the corporeal senses truly appear as integral experiences. The self . . . is compelled to make forms—including the forms of persons striving to represent their corporeal imaginations to others."

Whether thought has an ultimately and exclusively linguistic basis, whether language itself is primarily figurative, whether all language is, as Emerson claimed, fossil poetry, whether there is such a thing as "thinking in images" as opposed to "thinking in language," these fine-grained philosophical and linguistic and neurological arguments I will leave to those much more expertly informed. Whether the limits of my language are indeed the limits of my world I cannot prove; the limits of language do seem provisionally to set the outer reaches, however, of a poem's call to me and perhaps to you.

If a lion could speak, we would not understand him.
So wrote Wittgenstein, famously, in his *Philosophical Investigations*.

I cannot help but recall his gnomic pronouncement when I recall H.D.'s "Oread": if a mountain nymph could speak, would we understand her?

> *Whirl up sea—*
> *whirl your pointed pines . . .*

H.D.'s "Oread" displays and transforms the anthropomorphic, animating premise of apostrophe, that gesture so basic to lyric. (Viz. Shelley, in his "Ode to the West Wind": "Be thou me, Spirit fierce, my Spirit!")

The Oread is nymphomorphic, her subjectivity projected from and grounded in her mountain ground, its pine trees, its sensuous greens and stark rocks. Thus when she addresses the sea, commands the sea, provokes the sea to respond to her spell, she cannot help but invest the sea with her mountainous mind:

> splash your great pines
> on our rocks,
> hurl your green over us,
> cover us with your pools of fir.

Cover us with your pools of fir, your aqueous splash gone spiny, piney, and green.

H.D.'s incantation both displays and thwarts the standard anthropomorphic logic of projection basic to lyric and perhaps to human thinking; the poem may also be read as a brilliant anatomy of what Freud called "the omnipotence of thoughts." The fantasy that one's mind not only can do work in the world but indeed can animate the world—the animistic and fetishistic conviction that objects or natural elements *are alive*—this is the condition common to very young children and primitives, Freud argues, and of course, common to those who persist in the childish pursuit of art making.

And yet. And yet. As Susan Stewart observes and as Elaine Scarry so lovingly, carefully shows in *The Body in Pain*, we spend our lives relying on the near aliveness of nature and of the object world, taking for granted, when privileged, when secure, that the object world, which includes poems as much as tools or tables or computers, responsively answers to and as if by magic anticipates human needs, human desires. Any ar-

tifact, indeed any humanly prepared or transformed sub-
stance, bears within it not only the congealed labor Marx re-
minds us it does or the movement of thought Arendt tells us it
does but also a more generalized human well-wishing: Be well.
Sit in this chair. This chair knows and anticipates both the hu-
man need for rest and the contours of a resting human body.
Now shut the window. This window bespeaks and answers the
simultaneous desire for shelter and our love of light and a view.
Now read this poem. This poem bespeaks our desire to com-
mune, to hear and be heard, to make the chaos of inner feeling
not only sentient but sharable. This poem brings the murk of
inner corporeal urgencies into enunciation, as Susan Stewart
might put it. If a mountain nymph is a creature of fantasy, her
imagined subjectivity is no less compellingly spoken, bril-
liantly and economically thought, for that. A stranger may ad-
dress us across centuries, languages, countries, genders. An
object, an artifact, addresses us. We lend and are lent a voice,
a form. We may be addressed across species. A sympathetic
cognitive projection underlies the logic of address here—

Hurl your green over us—

and enacts that broader linguistic, discursive condition of
intersubjectivity about which Emile Benveniste wrote so illu-
minatingly years ago in his essay "Subjectivity in Language"
(1958). Regarding the reciprocal structure of personal pro-
nouns, "I" and "you," Benveniste observed, "This polarity of

persons is the fundamental condition in language, of which the process of communication, in which we share, is only a mere pragmatic consequence . . . The very terms we are using here, *I* and *you*, are not to be taken as figures but as linguistic forms indicating 'person.' It is a remarkable fact—but who would notice it, since it is so familiar?—that the 'personal pronouns' are never missing from among the signs of a language, no matter what its type, epoch, or region may be. A language without expression of person cannot be imagined."

I may be a mountain nymph. You may be the sea. To command you, to address you, I must think you. "I" must think "you." And yet even as I think you I interfuse you with my own nature—my pines, my fir, my rocks.

Or rather, "our rocks." Splash your great pines on our rocks. For another thing H.D.'s Oread suggests in her vocal gesture is that hers is a communally grounded subjectivity—she speaks for and from a collective mode of social being. We might say that in Marxian terms she summons the sea *as* a species being, as a mountain nymph speaking herself as a nymph among nymphs, one of a species of nymphs with similarly mountainous minds and desires for sea-brought inundation: Hurl your green over *us*. Cover *us* with your pools of fir.

•

Thus through a fictive creature, the problem and fact of shared and sharable sentience sings itself forth. The Oread does not "sing beyond the genius of the sea," as Wallace Stevens's singer does in his "Idea of Order at Key West": her utterance aspires precisely to sing the very particular genius of the sea—its capacity to respond, to whirl, splash, hurl, and cover, to inundate on command. Whether this is an invocation on the border of a desired annihilation, whether this is an incantation portending a violent lashing cleansing, we do not know. We might speculate that the Oread, here speaking for and implicitly with her sisters, calls on the sea to save-by-covering: according to legend, one Oread, Britomartis, threw herself into the sea to escape one of the predatory pursuers that perpetually trouble nymphs. Perhaps, we might speculate further, perhaps "Oread" might be read as a ritual re-enactment of that supplication, a remembering of that beneficent covering, that cloaking of the vulnerable subject in the medium of its choosing: *Cover us with your pools of fir.* We might recall too that Echo was an Oread, and might consider that H.D.'s "Oread" is a complex echoing of a primary mythico-lyric call. And here too we might recall Benveniste on personal pronouns, their logic of echo: "*I* posits another person, the one who . . . becomes my echo to whom I say *you* and says *you* to me" (225). The Oread is also an Auread, a hearing, a sympathetic responding to the sea, which precedes, as it were, the call. Here myth finds its "muthos," its saying. Here we might again invoke Wallace Stevens for a gloss on "Oread," for as Stevens wrote: "A mythology reflects its region . . . This raises the question of the image's truth. / The image must be of the nature of its creator" ("A Mythology Reflects Its Region"). Here, I would argue, H.D. has *thought* the preconditions of mythic saying and mythic imaging.

This may seem a lot of weight for an imagist poem to bear—though whether "Oread" truly is or remains an "imagist" or "vorticist" poem, as Pound first framed it, is interestingly arguable. There are of course many ways poems think about thinking, or about not-thinking. "Oread" presents a nondiscursive, phenomenologically oriented speech act. As a poem, it is barely, and yet decisively, there.

Stevens's "Man with the Blue Guitar" helps me think further about "the nature of the creator," this aspect of "Oread":

XXXVIII

I am a native in this world
And think in it as a native thinks,

Gesu, not native of a mind
Thinking the thoughts I call my own,

Native, a native in the world
And like a native think in it.

Like a native, H.D.'s Oread thinks. Like an Oread, a native of the mountain, the Oread is native in the world and like a native thinks in it.

This returns us to the remarkable capacity of lyric projection, its positing of nonhuman or marginally human natives who nevertheless might think as natives in our shared world. This can become an ethico-lyrical project, perhaps best exemplified for me in Wordsworth's early work, his powerful investigations in *Lyrical Ballads* of the thought of children, "idiots," vagrants, rustics, Native Americans, his sympathetic enactments of their thought over and against Coleridge's conviction that rustics, for example, didn't quite think. The most spectacular case of the sympathetic projection of thought may arise in Wordsworth's "Hart-Leap Well," a long ballad that begins as a conventional neomedievalizing chase, a story of one Sir Walter who hunts a hart and marvels at the hart's final leaps to its death: on that spot Sir Walter pledges to build a pleasure dome, a retreat for enjoyment and remembrance— not to recompense or memorialize the hart but to commemorate Sir Walter's savoring of its glorious leaps en route to its death. In contrast to Sir Walter's pleasure in the kill, we encounter in part II a typical Wordsworthian interlocutor, a shepherd who retells this story as the legendary lore, the backstory as it were, of this haunted place:

Some say that here a murder has been done,
And blood cries out for blood: but, for my part,
I've guess'd, when I've been sitting in the sun,
That it was all for that unhappy Hart.

What thoughts must through the creature's brain have pass'd!
From the stone on the summit of the steep
Are but three bounds, and look, Sir, at this last,
O Master! it has been a cruel leap.

("HART-LEAP WELL," LL. 137-44)

Remarkable here is not just the sympathy extended to a fellow creature in pain, a creature reimagined across centuries as exhausted and about to die, but the projection of thoughts into that creature's brain: What thoughts must through the creature's brain have passed! Here poetry announces that shared sentience, not the fact of shared language, will be the grounds of notionally shared thought. That the hart thought, the shepherd does not doubt; what specifically the hart thought, he cannot say: If a hart could speak, we would not understand him. Yet the broad contours of the hart's thought we can guess at, Wordsworth's shepherd suggests. We understand the hart's thought without the medium of language.

Haunted by a thinking hart, Wordsworth calls for the development of thinking human hearts, and in this ballad as in so many others he conducts an experiment in the nature of thought, its reach, its limitations.

Again, what intrigues me about Wordsworth's hart, and H.D.'s Oread, is that while they are obviously generated out of the anthropomorphic logic of *poiesis*—their sensuous, sentient human makers have clearly, humanly, made them—they nevertheless partly resist that logic. "For my thoughts are not your thoughts, neither are your ways my ways, saith the Lord" (Isaiah 55:8).

H.D.'s Oread and Wordsworth's hart and Margaret Cavendish's horribly hounded hare, poor Wat—all speaking or figured on the verge, their sentience on the edge of extinction—for me these figures are connate with the first "susceptible being" Wallace Stevens conjures in his poem "A Discovery of Thought" (1950), itself a poem of first lights, first sights, first thoughts, and first words:

> One thinks, when the houses of New England catch the first
>   sun,
>
> The first word would be of the susceptible being arrived,
> The immaculate disclosure of the secret no more obscured,
> The sprawling of winter might suddenly stand erect,
>
> Pronouncing its new life and ours, not autumn's prodigal
>   returned,

But an antipodal, far-fetched creature, worthy of birth,
The true tone of the metal of winter in what it says:

The accent of deviation in the living thing
That is its life preserved, the effort to be born
Surviving being born, the event of life.

The susceptible being arrived, a far-fetched creature, speaking in its own accent of deviation: this is one way to hear H.D.'s "Oread"—

• • • •

And those who have ears to hear will hear.

This is the sort of thing H.D. herself thought, as attested in one of her rare prose works on poetics: "Notes on Thought and Vision" (1919). She was hieratic, an elitist of the soul, though she had a democratic strain as well: "Anyone who wants can get through these stages today just as easily as the Eleusinian candidates outside Athens in the fifth century, B.C." (Just as easily!) Her notes on visionary initiation are occasionally slightly repulsive: "If your brain cannot stand the strain of following out these lines of thought, scientifically, and if you are not balanced and sane enough to grasp these things with a certain amount of detachment, you are obviously not ready for experiments in over-mind consciousness."

•

Well then!

And she invokes Socrates: "Today there are many wand-bearers but few inspired."

She was, she is, not wrong.

In the mid-1990s I would sometimes attend a University of Chicago colloquium on modernism. I thought of its very learned, very serious, very intense members as "the bearded male modernists," though only some had beards, and only some were male. On one occasion we were to discuss Yeats's "Leda and the Swan" alongside H.D.'s "Leda," with some recent critical essays as well. What I recall from that two-hour session, the last I attended, was a creeping feeling of horror, as it became clear that, whatever the intent of the programmers, the evening was devolving into a "who does rape better" discussion: and clearly, Yeats did rape better.

Touché!

It is hard for me these years later to disentangle my strong sense of the bad faith of the terms of that discussion from any reading of these poems. *Obviously*, one might say, *obviously* Yeats's "Leda and the Swan" is a *better* poem—if by "better" you mean memorable, wrought, impressive, titanic, influential, dialectical, linguistically and rhythmically virtuosic. And one could also shift the terrain here and say that whereas Yeats is wringing out of myth (and into myth) a world-historical shattering sonnet, H.D. is up to something else—tracking the phenomenology of a kind of benumbed erotic encounter, one that seems almost not to have happened:

> Where the slow river
> meets the tide,
> a red swan lifts red wings
> and darker beak,
> and underneath the purple down
> of his soft breast
> uncurls his coral feet . . .
>
> Ah kingly kiss—
> no more regret
> nor old deep memories
> to mar the bliss;
> where the low sedge is thick,
> the gold day-lily
> outspreads and rests
> beneath soft fluttering
> of red swan wings
> and the warm quivering
> of the red swan's breast.

One registers aspects of her typical lyric style: its hypnagogic state; the carefully paced phrasings, the predominance of slow, heavy monosyllables, the insinuating rhymes (kiss/ bliss, rests/breast, wings/quivering); the stationing of the poem at a border territory "where the slow river / meets the tide," the meeting here slow, aqueous, and obliviating— the kiss negating or surpassing "regret" and "old deep memories"; the action muted, literally and figuratively submerged, the strongest verbal forms the gerunds "fluttering" and "quivering"—"quivering" a recurring word in H.D.'s erotic lexicon (as in "the passion / quivering yet to break" in her "Fragment Thirty-six").

As I recall, the charge against H.D.—and it was also of course the charge against the scholars who had worked hard to rehabilitate her reputation, in the by-now familiar yet no less praiseworthy terms of feminist recuperation—included this: her evasion of real *stuff*, of history, violence, difficulty, the world: her evasion of everything Pound, for example, embraced. (That this was a comparison that for some would tip the scales for H.D. did not occur to this crew.) She did not *put on his knowledge with his power*. Condescension would morph quickly into contempt for the woman who *let her wealthy lesbian lover support her*, the woman who *founded no movements*, who *edited no journals*, who apparently lazily glided around Europe *entre les deux guerres* in a twee supine daze, her only claim to fame her association with More Important (or rather Actually Important) Artists and perhaps her later, brief analysis with Freud.

It is interesting how often one is expected to be *for* something and simultaneously *against* something else. The both-and falls away, so too the neither-nor.

> *My mind is divided;*
> *I know not what to do.*
> (SAPPHO)

> *Neither honey nor bee for me.*
> (SAPPHO)

And it is true that H.D. swims in some murky waters, and that after the first toughened hard-soft, sweet-bitter Imagist lyrics her poems are often slack—

and it is true that, as my love said upon reading H.D.'s "Leda," one might well respond, "Well, isn't it slightly ridiculous?— 'Ah kingly kiss'??!"

And one could say as well that it is all too typical of her verse to collapse into a kind of postcoital inertia, nothing *to mar the bliss*, no blow or burst of thought or rhythm to interrupt *the warm quivering / of the red swan's breast.*

All this could be said.

And also: *Whirl up sea!*

And also: *Heu, it whips round my ankles!*

● ● ● ●

Much of the force of great modernist works arises from their desublimating impulse channeled into shatteringly, newly adequate forms—their fuck you, here it is, take it for all in all, we shall not be constrained by gentility, there will be swagger sex and frying liver and shitting and ads and trams and masturbating and shell shock and newspaper datelines and porous consciousness and airplanes and abortions and cross-dressers and drumming Negroes and tragic Sapphic liaisons, etc.—

H.D. thought D. H. Lawrence's later poems not sublimated enough. She rejected them entirely. One might find a poem like "Leda" entirely too sublimated. More broadly, her mythic tool kit, her cultural surfing moving ever to the fore in the later work, is for some readers an impediment—what is all this Egyptian stuff, not to mention the ongoing repertoire of Greek figures, masks, and plots: *Why not say what happened?* as Robert Lowell came to ask.

This perhaps marks an impoverished sense of "what happens."

•

Where H.D. is like Yeats for me, is like my memory of the first impact of Dylan Thomas's "Fern Hill" on me, is like Donne's "Batter My Heart" for me, is like certain stanzas and lyrics in Shelley for me, is like Sappho, is indeed often My Sappho, is in her bodily force—

her kinesthetics of transmission—

for some of her poems bypassed my brain and registered directly on the nerve endings.

All these poets have had for me a distinctly somatic power. One could say they cast a spell—albeit different spells.

Thus

        though I sang in my chains like the sea—

there was a ringing

        up so many floating bells down

and I wondered

        what had that flower to do with being white?

and trembled, for

> what but design of darkness to appall
> if design govern in a thing so small

and found myself

> turning and turning in the widening gyre

and knew

> my mind is reft

and said

> my soul is an enchanted boat
> born on the silver waves of thy sweet singing

and faltered as

> strain upon strain,
> sound surging upon sound
> makes my brain blind

and I found myself

> nor ever chaste except you ravish me—

I sat on a narrow bed in an English house I read in a large book and found *sound surging upon sound / making my brain blind— O I am eager for you!*

●

To talk about H.D. is almost inevitably to talk about sexuality—not least because she so often invites it, particularly in the poems titled after Sapphic fragments. To adopt Sappho's mask is to invite the sexual inquiry that Sappho's name itself marks. "Sappho has become for us a name, an abstraction as well as a pseudonym" (H.D., *The Wise Sappho*).

My Sappho begins with H.D.
Or perhaps my Sappho begins with Pound:

> Spring . . .
> Too long . . .
> Gongyla . . .
> **("LUSTRA")**

A ring of girls dancing, a chorus—what Sappho legendarily led. I do not have *a beautiful little girl* I did not have a strange vision of picture-writing in 1919 while on the Scilly Isles with my lover I did not survive influenza and give birth and outlive the wreck of my marriage and the Great War and live to write a long epic in another war—
H.D. did.

• • • •

To think about H.D. is to think, eventually, about Freud.
For theirs was a conjunction.

"She is perfect . . . *only she has lost her spear*"—what Freud, "the Master," says to H.D., as she recalls it in *Tribute to Freud*. It is 1933 and she has come to Vienna to study with the great old god, the founder of a new religion, the braver of mysteries: Freud. They share a deep love of antiquity; he knows archaic Greece to be her imaginative homeland. He has shown her a small figure, a statue of Nike—one of the many ancient treasures and fragments adorning his office.

She is perfect, only she has lost her spear.

A rather leaden point, this, if we choose to take it a certain way (and H.D. did)—the goddess, and the woman poet, missing (lacking) the phallus.

To talk about poetry is for some to talk about therapy and psychoanalysis.

Perhaps it stinks of the twentieth century, this enmeshing of poetry and psychoanalysis, or of poetry and the psychotherapeutic.

When I was in therapy I sometimes talked about what I was reading, what I was writing, and it was natural that I should mention H.D. and the long essay I was then writing on the relationship of H.D. and Freud, and more broadly on that between poetics and psychoanalysis.

"Put H.D. in the place of Sigmund Freud" (*Tribute to Freud*). As the analysts tell you, as Freud told H.D., there are always

multiple causes for any one thing—events are "overdeter-
mined." And there are no accidents.

So it was no accident that I was fixated on this relationship as—

> I did not know how to differentiate
> between volcanic desire,
> anemones like embers
> and purple fire
> of violets
> like red heat,
> and the cold
> silver
> of her feet:
>
> I had two loves separate;
> God who loves all mountains,
> alone knew why
> and understood . . .
>
> ("THE MASTER")

as I was riven—

> I know not what to do,
> my mind is reft:

as I had lain in a bed wondering—

> Shall I break your rest,
> devouring, eager? . . .

Shall I turn and take
comfortless snow within my arms?
press lips to lips
that answer not,
press lips to flesh
that shudders not nor breaks?

as I would later lie in a bed next to the beloved, incandescent,
indecisive—

I know not what to do:
strain upon strain,
sound surging upon sound
makes my brain blind;
as a wave-line may wait to fall
yet (waiting for its falling)
still the wind may take
from off its crest,
white flake on flake of foam,
that rises,
seeming to dart and pulse
and rend the light,
so my mind hesitates
above the passion
quivering yet to break,
so my mind hesitates
above my mind,
listening to song's delight.

as earlier in a rented room in Washington, D.C., I had lain anguished awake next to my husband, who also lay there anguished awake—

> I was not dull and dead when I fell
> back on our couch at night.
> I was not indifferent when I turned
> and lay quiet.
> I was not dead in my sleep.
>
> **("FRAGMENT FORTY-ONE")**

And when my husband's brother said to me in a dark bar one night, "So it's the bisexual thing that's the reason for the divorce—?" and the bones of my face turned to ash—
Could I not have said—

> I have had enough—
> . . . .
> O to blot out this garden
> to forget, to find a new beauty
> in some terrible
> wind-tortured place.
>
> **("SHELTERED GARDEN")**

Might I have said—

> Splintered the crystal of identity,
> shattered the vessel of integrity . . .
>
> **("THE WALLS DO NOT FALL")**

Could I have thought—

> I compensate my soul
> with a new role
> ("SIGIL")

Did I really feel—

> This is my own world,
> these can't see . . .
> ("SIGIL")

Could I have predicted—

> That will be me,
> silver
> and wild and free;
>
> that will be me
> to send a shudder through you,
> cold wind
>
> through an aspen tree
> ("SIGIL")

•   •   •   •

I have thought of her in a bedsit in England, in a studio in Chicago, in a cabin in New Hampshire; I have thought of her by seashores, by lakes, and inland; I may think of her in future

years when I discover what sears and what wanes in places I
cannot yet know—

no motion has she now, nor force, yet she has motion and force;
she is of the *rocks and stones and trees*; she is of the sung mind—

Let us *bring her an offering*, let us

> dare more than the singer
> offering her lute,
> the girl her stained veils,
> the woman her swathes of birth . . .
>
> ("FRAGMENT FORTY-ONE")

Let us say that like Sappho, H.D. "has become for us a name,
an abstraction as well as a pseudonym for poignant human
feeling, she is indeed rocks set in a blue sea, she is the sea it-
self, breaking and tortured and torturing, but never broken"
(*The Wise Sappho*).

Let us say

> we have a song,
> on the bank we share our arrows;

O let us say then—

> She is great,
> we measure her by the pine trees.
>
> ("MOONRISE")

9.

MY TRANSLATED

AN ABECEDARY

My Adelia Prado is Ellen Doré Watson.

My Akhmatova is Judith Hemschemeyer.

My Alberto Caeiro is Fernando Pessoa.

My Alcaeus is David A. Campbell.

My Taha Muhammed Ali is Peter Cole, Yahya Hijazi, and
Gabriel Levin.

My Álvaro de Campos is Pessoa.

My Anne Carson is Anne Carson.

My poetry of Arab Andalusia and my Hebrew poetry of Muslim
and Christian Spain is Peter Cole.

My Archilochus is Douglas E. Gerber and Guy Davenport.

My Bashō, my Issa, my Buson, are Robert Hass.

My Bashō is also Nobuyuki Yuasa.

My Baudelaire is Louise Varèse, as is my Rimbaud.

My *Beowulf* is Seamus Heaney.

My Bible is King James, which means much Tyndale.

My Blaise Cendrars is Ron Padgett.

My *Book of Songs* (*Shi jing*) is Arthur Waley, despite.

My Brodsky is Joseph Brodsky, perhaps unfortunately.

My Cavafy is still Rae Dalven.

My Celan is unsurprisingly John Felstiner.

My René Char is many.

My Inger Christensen is Susanna Nied.

My Dahlia Ravikovitch is Chana Bloch and Chana Kronfeld.

My Dante is Dorothy Sayers, still.

My Mahmoud Darwish is Fady Joudah and also Catherine Cobham and Sinan Antoon.

My Eugenio Montale is Jonathan Galassi.

My Federico García Lorca is a vast field of devotion including W. S. Merwin, Stephen Spender, and Lysander Kemp.

My French poets are often Keith Waldrop or Rosemarie Waldrop or Pierre Joris.

My Durs Grünbein is Michael Hofmann.

My Ho Xuan Huong is John Balaban.

My Homer is Richmond Lattimore, despite Fitzgerald, and is sometimes Christopher Logue, Alice Oswald, and Pope.

My Horace is Joseph Clancy and sometimes David Ferry.

My Inanna, Queen of Heaven and Earth, is Diane Wolkstein and Samuel Noah Kramer.

My Ivan Wernisch is Jonathan Bolton.

My Juvenal is Peter Green and John Dryden and Samuel Johnson.

My Jorge Luis Borges is Efraín Kristal and Stephen Kessler and Richard Wilbur.

My Kabir is Arvind Krishna Mehrotra.

My language poets are other language poets.

My Giacomo Leopardi is Jonathan Galassi.

My Li Po is sometimes Ezra Pound.

My Mandelstam is Clarence Brown and W. S. Merwin.

My Mimnermos is Anne Carson.

My Nicanor Parra is Liz Werner.

My Omar Khayyám is Edward Fitzgerald.

My Paul Muldoon is Paul Muldoon.

My Pessoa is Richard Zenith.

My Psalms are Allen Ginsberg and before him Whitman.

My Pushkin does not exist.

My Raymond Queneau is most likely to be Teo Savory.

My Reverdy is Ron Padgett.

My Ricardo Reis is Pessoa.

My Rilke is Stephen Mitchell, irrevocably.

My Robert Burns is Robert Burns.

My Sappho is Jim Powell and sometimes David A. Campbell
    and occasionally Anne Carson and less often H.D. and Olga
    Broumas.

My Sextus Propertius is Ezra Pound and also Vincent Katz and
    sometimes Devin Johnston.

My Song of Songs is Chana Bloch and Ariel Bloch when not
    King James.

My Sophocles is David Grene and Seamus Heaney and Dudley
    Fitts and Robert Fitzgerald and Elizabeth Wyckoff.

My Georg Trakl is Daniel Simko.

My Tsvetayeva is Elaine Feinstein.

My Ko Un is Brother Anthony of Taizé and Young-Moo Kim and Gary Gach.

My Ungaretti is Andrew Frisardi.

My Virgil is Robert Fitzgerald.

My Wang Wei is David Hinton.

My Wisława Szymborska is Clare Cavanagh and Stanisław Barańczak and Joanna Trzeciak.

My Xue Tao is Jeanne Larsen.

My Yannis Ritsos is Edmund Keeley and sometimes Kimon Friar.

My Yehuda Amichai is Stephen Mitchell and Chana Bloch and Chana Kronfeld thus far.

My Zbigniew Herbert is still despite Alissa Valles's recent great efforts John and Bogdana Carpenter, with occasional appearances by Peter Dale Scott and Czesław Miłosz.

My Robert Zimmerman is Bob Dylan.

10

MY LOUISE GLÜCK

The studio is larger than a studio; though you sleep on a fold-out futon that you do not fold out, there is a separate room with a kitchen and a small table, one you've bought for yourself by yourself not with or for him from whom you'll soon be divorced. The book is on the table, its green cover is open, and you're reading and there it is, the shock of an answering tone:

> The great thing
> is not having
> a mind. Feelings:
> oh, I have those; they
> govern me. I have
> a lord in heaven
> called the sun, and open
> for him, showing him
> the fire of my own heart, fire
> like his presence.

What could such glory be
if not a heart? Oh my brothers and sisters,
were you like me once, long ago,
before you were human? Did you
permit yourselves
to open once, who would never
open again? Because in truth
I am speaking now
the way you do. I speak
because I am shattered.

("THE RED POPPY")

From *The Wild Iris*: a kind of lieder cycle, as Helen Vendler put it, a book of poems unembarrassed to activate the oldest, most basic lyric tropes and to sidle up to a god who might be addressed or spoken through as if he existed, as if he too were given to wonder over the tragicomic human venture, every paradise lost. Flowers, seasons, trees, the wind, longing, loss, an endlessly mythified garden: this is the stuff of the book.

The book should have failed; there are many other poets who traffic in this material and it is dreadful—forced engagement with nature, revolting rhetorical performances of the pathetic fallacy (I feel for you! You, Nature, Feel for and with Me!), the strenuousness of it all, an anti-intellectual officially celebratory or officially depressed lyricism, a bourgeois narcissism tricked out in the outworn creed of a discredited romanticism.

You know a lot, too much perhaps, about discredited romanticism.
Not to mention bourgeois narcissism.

Glück writes in her essay "Education of the Poet": "It seems to me that the idea of lawlessness is a romance, and romance is what I most struggle to be free of."

Feelings: / oh, I have those; they / govern me.
They governed me.
But insufficiently.

One should not move, should not act, in a state of crippling ambivalence. There is a lower and a higher ambivalence, the first the condition of unexpressed congealed emotional tension, the other the mature fruit of a long-considered looking at the case.

Wholehearted, wholehearted! That is all you longed to be. Everything would be sacrificed for that. Not least your marriage.

And rightly so.
You thought.
And still think.

I couldn't do it again,
I can hardly bear to look at it—

in the garden, in light rain
the young couple planting
a row of peas, as though
no one has ever done this before,
the great difficulties have never as yet
been faced and solved—

They cannot see themselves,
in fresh dirt, starting up
without perspective . . .

("THE GARDEN")

The philosopher Alain Badiou asserts, in his "Fifteen Theses on Contemporary Art": "I think the great question about contemporary art is how not to be Romantic."

Schiller famously distinguished between "the naive" and "the sentimental," with moderns fated to be sentimental in their art and consciousness—precisely because they, unlike those who lived in naive epochs, *were conscious*, divided, reflective, capable of producing and thus required to produce an art of secondary process.

Glück reanimates the naive—the speaking flower, the responsive wind—through the governing consciousness Schiller called "sentimental." Schiller's "sentimental" (*sentamenta-lisch*) does not quite align with our contemporary sense of "sentimental"—his is closer to an achieved irony regarding the human condition.

Incredible the pathos of the sentimental submitting to the askesis of the naive: the asking of the elemental questions, the touching of the basic tones, without forgoing the rigors of thought:

> Oh my brothers and sisters,
> were you like me once, long ago,
> before you were human?

An anatomy of feeling, of mind, with voice the suture between them, all conducted through a colloquy of voices: an imagined poppy, a trillium, snowdrops, sometimes a woman, sometimes a god or "lord" or divine creator—this last figure often bemused, frustrated by ongoing human resistance and constriction, the inability to move beyond all-too-human limitation:

> And all this time
> I indulged your limitation, thinking
>
> you would cast it aside yourselves sooner or later,
> thinking matter could not absorb your gaze forever . . .
>
> I cannot go on
> restricting myself to images

because you think it is your right
to dispute my meaning:

I am prepared now to force
clarity upon you.

("CLEAR MORNING")

And then the nonhuman sentient speakers of *The Wild Iris*, the flowers who speak to the human condition more precisely because outside it, and who are thus required compulsively to analogize, to wonder:

> Oh my brothers and sisters,
> were you like me once, long ago,
> before you were human? Did you
> permit yourselves
> to open once, who would never
> open again? Because in truth
> I am speaking now
> the way you do. I speak
> because I am shattered.

I am speaking now / the way you do.

The Wild Iris explores the great power of mind, its titanic *as if*: *as if* flowers could speak, gods respond, the wind give voice. As if everything sentient could find its way toward an articulate speech a human could understand. As if the shattering everywhere in the world might create its own communal lyric—not only, not merely, the shattering of romances, gardens, expectations, ideals, but the simple terrible tearing of a petal; the burning of a field of wheat.

I am speaking now / the way you do.

And the realizing that there is in fact no assured pathway through a merely human speech.

> you would never accept
>
> a voice like mine, indifferent
> to the objects you busily name . . .
>
> **("CLEAR MORNING")**

The address rings in a void. She calls the addressee god. It might be a birch. It is unresponsive. It could be anyone:

> I see it is with you as with the birches:
> I am not to speak to you
> in the personal way. Much
> has passed between us.
>
> **("MATINS")**

Tacking between the deliverance of the message and its going awry, between communicating and not communicating, beyond communication—

I speak / because I am shattered.

•

Riven, what would you divest, the body or the mind? *The great thing / is not having / a mind.* Not to have to think of it. *Not to think of what I needs must feel* (Coleridge, "Dejection: An Ode"). The bitter exhilaration of negation. The blithe announcement of de-mentation: sentience, not thought. Feelings, *oh, I have those,* faux-casually invoked and put in their syntactical place even as the Poppy acknowledges "they govern me."

> You hear this voice? This is my mind's voice;
> you can't touch my body now.
> It has changed once, it has hardened,
> don't ask it to respond again.
>
> **("AVERNO")**

This from a later book, *Averno,* a book of "negative creation" that reworks Glück's ongoing inquiry into incarnation, discarnation.

In those earlier days you were also reading Elaine Scarry, *The Body in Pain*: "to have a body is to be describable, creatable, alterable, and woundable."
I speak / because I am shattered.

When "but to think is to be full of sorrow" (Keats), when every thought became a laceration, when thought itself—your anchor, your bane—became a weapon, when to breathe was to gasp and to walk to stumble—

there was this answering ferocity, authoritative, beyond its undergone great grief. Small exquisite songs in a minor key, the world taken within and pondered and exhaled, transformed by a sensitive sentience.

Louise Glück's *Wild Iris* was a companion more intimate than any living friend, a murmur and rasp and balm in the mind those months the structures of living you yourself had erected were now collapsing, the foundations battered by you yourself. Your depression was florid, ardent, a sick fever of desired annihilation when any flicker of energy served only to fuel and intensify despair. That you were fully aware of the cognitive gaps in your convictions, that you were in fact far more robust than you knew, that you suspected this, that understanding offered no cure for suffering, that from several all-too-obvious angles your maniacal self-involvement and endless therapy hours were further proof that consciousness as you pursued it was a luxury, and disgusting—

The Wild Iris is an outrageous experiment in the pathetic fallacy, undertaken without renouncing critique.

•

Love is an outrageous experiment in the pathetic fallacy, the machinery of projection—O let us call it hope, let us call it trust, let us call it desire—set in motion so the space between lovers might vibrate. The anxiety about and for the other: Do you feel as I do? Do I know how you feel? Do your words align with your feelings, your thoughts? Does your body respond in tune? Are we in tune? Do you know yourself? How shall I know you? How shall I know if I know you?

How shall I know if I know myself if all I know is that I do not know?

The great thing / is not having / a mind.

> . . . I didn't know my voice
> if one were given me
> would be so full of grief, my sentences
> like cries strung together.
> I didn't even know I felt grief
> until that word came, until I felt
> rain streaming from me.
>
> ("TRILLIUM")

One moves to the things behind words, nominalism exploded, the feeling attendant upon the word that gives a hard knowing—

•

Poetry: to help us feel that which we perceive, and to imagine that which we know: Shelley.

All those years vulnerable to the upsurge of a feeling hardened to a governing thought: I wish I were dead—

which modulated into a definitive statement: I am dead.

The Jungians call this the *nigredo state*; they borrow here as elsewhere from the alchemists, whom one can approach as giving us "metaphors for living," as Yeats said in other context of his mystic inspirators. In the Vale of Soulmaking, in alchemical process, the soul passes through this blackened, fragmented, provisionally dead state, where all is stasis—

what Keats so indelibly traced in his "Ode to a Nightingale," when he inters himself, proleptically buries himself. "Still wouldst thou sing, and I have ears in vain— / To thy high requiem become a sod."

The nigredo state enacts a descendental revelation: here you are, dismembered, buried:

> At the end of my suffering
> there was a door.

Hear me out: that which you call death
I remember.

Overhead, noises, branches of the pine shifting.
Then nothing. The weak sun
flickered over the dry surface.

It is terrible to survive
as consciousness
buried in the dark earth.—

("THE WILD IRIS")

Buried consciousness. This was your body.
To thy high requiem become a sod.

This was your first encounter with a characteristic element of
Glück's work, at least in those books after *The Wild Iris*: her
experiments in posthumous enunciation.

Hear me out: that which you call death
I remember.

("THE WILD IRIS")

And from her book *Averno*:

I think I can remember
being dead.

("PERSEPHONE THE WANDERER")

Death here is the limit-case of sentience, and the strange negative space out of which a new kind of enunciation emerges:

> I heard a fly buzz—when I died—

Perhaps the most brilliant and relentless explorer of this liminal zone, this posthumous condition that generates an uncanny aliveness in voice and mind, is Emily Dickinson—

> This is the Hour of Lead—
> Remembered, if outlived,
> As Freezing persons, recollect the Snow—
> First—Chill—then Stupor—then the letting go—
>
> (372)

> Because I could not stop for Death—
> He kindly stopped for me—
> The Carriage held but just Ourselves—
> And Immortality.
> . . . .
> Since then—'tis Centuries—and yet
> Feels shorter than the Day
> I first surmised the Horses' Heads
> Were toward Eternity—
>
> (479)

> I died for Beauty—but was scarce
> Adjusted in the Tomb

When One who died for Truth, was lain
In an adjoining Room—

He questioned softly "Why I failed"?
"For Beauty", I replied—
"And I—for Truth—Themself are One—
We Brethren, are", He said—

And so, as Kinsmen, met a Night—
We talked between the Rooms—
Until the Moss had reached our lips—
And covered up—Our names—

(448)

This homely colloquy among the dead—a parody of a genteel conversation that could happen in any Amherst parlor—points to Keats, self-laid in the tomb of his imagined death, addressing the nightingale: "still wouldst thou sing, and I have ears in vain— / To thy high requiem become a sod."

Badiou: "I think the great question about contemporary art is how not to be Romantic."

At the end of my suffering
there was a door.

Hear me out: that which you call death
I remember.

Some complain, Adam Kirsch perhaps most trenchantly, that Glück's work is programmatically morbid, the limited intonations of a rigid depressive. She is, according to Jordan Davis, a *big neg*. This seems to me tellingly wrong. It mistakes apparent content for emotional disposition, and indicts the work by an attitude about the latter. When Glück's work fails, as it sometimes does for me, the hieratic manner so amazingly earned hardens, and feels willed. She has written strikingly on will, and she knows profoundly whereof she writes, anorexia a syndrome in which a person not yet in contact with herself struggles to produce herself via efforts of will. One who survived such a long youthful apprenticeship to what are clearly her own formidable powers of will is best prepared to limn its limitations: "The dream of art is not to assert what is already known but to illuminate what has been hidden, and the path to the hidden world is not inscribed by will" ("Education of the Poet").

• • • •

Years ago you'd gone to Bennington for a week, listened to readings in a large fragrant barn, its steps and rafters filled with the ardent open-eared, all attending to a southern novelist, a woman who in her reading reminded you about what you too rarely thought about—the sheer tidal pleasures of fiction unfolding aloud in time: a sensuous story about a spirited teen girl with a low-down home life and a sexual initiation real or imagined or wanted with a charismatic preacher. Even to distill it thus is to falsen it, as we've all heard this kind of story from that kind of novelist, but she magicks us and all hold their breath at the end—

a pause—

a loud communal exhale—

among those listening nearby a handsome poet a Vietnam vet who now turns and says commanding attention *Now there's a woman writer who really likes men.*

—A million hallucinated adversaries seemingly slain in his glaring peacock eyes—

> I never turned anyone into a pig.
> Some people are pigs; I make them
> look like pigs.
> ("CIRCE'S POWER")

This from her book *Meadowlands*. Her authority is undeniably, frighteningly female, but not only. This provokes the usual range of responses, defenses, adulations.

•

After this reading another poet mused on Sharon Olds, her first books. Of *Satan Says*: "Well, when that came out we were impressed. We didn't know she had that in her."

What stunned: the casual magisterial excluding *we*.

He told a story of going to a reading featuring several poets, Glück among them—there she was, following another poet, a genial, jokey comic fellow who left that vibe behind him in the room. And she got up with her narrow shoulders and a severe expression and launched:

> It is not the moon, I tell you.
> It is these flowers
> lighting the yard.
>
> I hate them.
> I hate them as I hate sex,
> the man's mouth
> sealing my mouth, the man's
> paralyzing body—
>
> and the cry that always escapes,
> the low, humiliating
> premise of union—
>
> ("MOCK ORANGE")

and all the air went out of the room.

To empty a room of its air like that. To annihilate its complacence.

These are perhaps low ambitions, to have that kind of command, that kind of authority, perhaps always reactive, always defensive. These may not be properly "aesthetic" responses: they are not disinterested, they are saturated with merely personal emotion, hope, grudge, resentment, joy in an unforeseen triumph. Yet out of this stew something more permanent and purged may come forth.

In the mid-1990s you were sitting in 57th Street Books in Chicago, one of Hyde Park's landmark bookstores, having leafed through several books and chosen one: Glück's *Proofs and Theories: Essays on Poetry*. The cool surgical gaze turned again and again on oneself; the exacting account of the poet's education; the anorexia, the analysis, the maniacal protective ecstasies of refusal and then refusing refusal—

Well I see you are reading Louise.

He'd come in, the famous novelist following the bookstore employee encumbered by fifteen volumes of the novelist's latest. Let us pass over his name in silence, he so presumptuously familiar with names. In your book group the women with ties to publishing and book fairs and signings had been cooing the previous week over his *amazing blue eyes*.

Yes they are amazing.

Yes I am reading Ms. Glück.

And with no invitation he unspools how she married for this and divorced for that and how the long-ago affair with this one blew up—

Slam the book.
You didn't.
Incredulity rooted you to your seat. That, and curiosity. What would he not say?

Dear Ms. Glück,
This is just a note to say that if you consider R—— F—— a friend, he is not.
Sincerely,
An Admirer

A note you never sent.

Never to meet them, only to read them.

• • • •

Yeats wrote a dialogue of self and soul. Do we have souls any-more? The soul persists in Glück's repertoire of nouns. Some would find in that the mark of an unpurged romanticism: still singing the songs of oneself! An incredibly narrow self! The soul! I was in therapy and paid to have a dream life I then had a dream life I was in the Vale of Soulmaking I paid to have a soul:

> Sometimes a man or woman forces his despair
> on another person, which is called
> baring the heart, alternatively, baring the soul—
> meaning for this moment they acquired souls—
> outside, a summer evening, a whole world
> thrown away on the moon . . .
>
> **("LOVE IN MOONLIGHT")**

Glück writes that after each book, she moves stringently to ward something else in the next: "Each book I've written has culminated in a conscious diagnostic act, a swearing off" ("Education of the Poet"). After her second book: "I wanted to learn a longer breath. And to write without the nouns central to that second book; I had done everything I could do with *moon* and *pond.*"

Is there anything still to be done with *soul*? See *Averno*:

> The assignment was to fall in love.
> The author was female.
> The ego had to be called the soul.
>
> ("PRISM")

O let us swear off these miserable plots, these determining nouns, this *soul*, and *love*, and *woman*, this revolting *poetry* I too dislike, this disgusting *I*—

> Not I, you idiot, not self, but we, we—waves
> of sky blue like
> a critique of heaven: why
> do you treasure your voice
> when to be one thing
> is to be next to nothing?
>
> ("SCILLA")

Sunk in the earth become a sod could one not stay there forever beyond all sounding all voicing all caring—

> I can't hear your voice
> for the wind's cries, whistling over the bare ground
>
> I no longer care
> what sound it makes

when I was silenced, when did it first seem
pointless to describe that sound

what it sounds like can't change what it is . . .

("OCTOBER")

Sunk in the tomb of your stupid self you could not but agree
that *the great question about contemporary art is how not to be
Romantic.* The great question of a life.

> I stood
> at the doorway,
> ridiculous as it now seems.

("OCTOBER")

AT THE END, A DOOR

I walked through

and on the other side
I thought I'd look back

through the door
"that was another life"

here I am
on this side standing looking

same life

What for
this failure

the outline
of the beloved

body haunting sleep
fleshing itself out of nothing

what for this failure love

Romance is what I most struggle to be free of.
It is terrible to survive / as consciousness / buried in the dark earth.

Yet

let them
do their worst, let them
bury me with the Romantics,
their pointed yellow leaves
falling and covering me.

("MATINS")

11

MY FANNY HOWE

INTIMATIONS

It is cold in Chicago, as cold as it gets in the Boston winters chilling Fanny Howe's poems. If you live near the lake, as I did, there are few trees to slow the wind as it blows down from Canada over the Great Lakes as if by invitation through the cracks where the joints of your window frames don't quite meet. There is an inner and an outer weather. Sometimes they align, and sometimes that is good—as in that summer you were wholly gripped by love, and the road lined with chicory and Queen Anne's lace became the road of desire leading to the palace of fulfillment. But there are also seasons so blasting that the heart withers and nearly fails, and despite your dislike for Matthew Arnold, or rather for late-twentieth-century boosters who look to poetry to "save us," as if we could be saved, as if we were designed to be saved, and perhaps we are—despite your suspicion not only of salvation but also of consolation, there is a poem or rather a pitched voice that brings forth a music you would make if you could make music—

> My bedclothes were stuffed with ashes
> The spreads were incarnadine
>
> Our match had burned at both ends
> Since temptation concludes where the middle is nothing
>
> Can a desire be a mistake?
> The theme can be wrong, but not the music
>
> And I lay there dying
> For my asylum
>
> Was myself

("THE QUIETIST")

For my asylum was myself: a balm and a curse—to find oneself, and only oneself, the refuge. Self-sufficiency, self-torture. Perhaps that is why "I lay there dying."

So a poem like the self could offer a difficult asylum. Not the glorious intricate stanzas, the little rooms of Petrarch or the Metaphysical poets, but the starkly sounding line, the essential couplet, the morphemes and phonemes and incremental motions of the soul's investigation, the sigh and the cry of the *I*—and I lay there dying, for my asylum was myself.

•

One seeks asylum because one finds oneself a refugee, endangered: one is attempting to flee violence. To flee intimacy, its violence; the self, its violence; the body, its violence; the family, its violence; money, its violence; race, its violence; the state, its violence. Yet in these poems you find a refusal to turn away even as they seek asylum. A refusal to participate in the sick fictions of success or easy safety. But also a wish to relieve one's own sharpness, to lighten the burden of being "a seasoned witness" ("The End," 26). A cleaving to a certain freedom:

> To be free of the need
> to make a waste of money
> when my passion,
> first and last,
> is for the ecstatic lash
> of the poetic line
>
> and no visible recompense.
>
> ("POEM FROM A SINGLE PALLET")

FANNY HOWE FOR THE PERPLEXED

There was a dispute you conducted, a basic quarrel with yourself, although it often took the form of a quarrel with others:

What to make of limits? Of disappointment? What was essen-
tial? Was it time to draw yourself within the limits of the firm
lines life was drawing around you? To make yourself a clear
figure, a discernible outline in the world? "What to make of a
diminished thing," sings Robert Frost's ovenbird. A friend
had quoted that once, as if to fortify you into a kind of stoic
acceptance. But you were never good at acceptance.

> The limits have wintered me
> as if white trees were there to be written on.

> It must be purgatory
> there are so many letters and things.

> Faith, hope and charity rise in the night
> like the stations of an accountant.

> And I remember my office, sufficiency.
>
> ("O'CLOCK")

But what would suffice? And wherein lies sufficiency? How to
survive one's own blighting eye?

> The stains of blackberries near Marx's grave
> do to color what eyes do to everything.
> Help me survive my own presence, open to the elements.
>
> ("O'CLOCK")

FANNY HOWE FOR UNBELIEVERS

He sleeps on the top of a mast, Elizabeth Bishop's unbeliever in "The Unbeliever," as does John Bunyan's before her. In the midst of doubt, besieged by waves, the pilgrim undertakes her difficult progress. Howe's unbeliever, her Veteran, offers an anti-credo, a litany of disbelief, the askesis to which we submit until we arrive at not a ground for belief but the movement of wind:

> I don't believe in ashes; some of the others do.
> I don't believe in better or best; some of the others do . . .
>
> I don't believe in seeking sheet music
> by Boston Common on a snowy day, don't believe
> in the lighting of malls seasonally . . .
>
> . . . Like a sweetheart
> of the iceberg or wings lost at sea
>
> the wind is what I believe in,
> the One that moves around each form
>
> ("VETERAN")

That dance between something and nothing. Between the One and the many. Between the frame and the view. Between the play of the mind and the pulse of the senses. Between belief and doubt. Between Alsace and Lorraine, Boston and San Diego, Mexico and the United States. Between sufficiency and ecstasy. Between anarchy and the rhythmic order called forth by love. Between anarchy and the jagged forms called forth by attention. Between song and silence.

> I have backed up
> into my silence
>
> as inexhaustible as the sun
> that calls a tip of candle
> to its furnace.
>
> Red sparks hit a rough surface.
> I have been out—cold—too—long enough.
>
> **("O'CLOCK")**

Red sparks hit a rough surface: The self, the song, an ignited match. The lyric of potential. The lyric of waste. The dashes of Dickinson.

Wordsworth's lyrics sing the praises of solitude, those occasions when the stores of thought return for private delectation, when treasured images

> flash upon that inward eye
> which is the bliss of solitude
>
> **("I WANDERED LONELY AS A CLOUD")**

You find in Howe both an inward and an outward eye. Lyric may require solitude but most often you find in Howe's poems not the bliss but the agony of solitude. Before her solitudes, behind them, lies a sundering, an impasse. Howe the lyric surgeon is looking to suture these gaps with the threads of her lines.

You find in these intimate lines an astonishing impersonality, not the impersonality T. S. Eliot advised the poet to cultivate but the impersonality of Zen. "Consciousness has nothing to do with me either / I'm just moving inside it, catch as catch can't" ("Introduction to the World").

FANNY HOWE THE UNSPARING AND UNSPARED

If Howe's poems bring you to speak of song and self, of asylum and attention, they bring you to speak as well of terror, a muse as good and as necessary as any other.

> There is a city of terror where
> they kill civilians outside
>
> restaurants—guys
> who are fathers and things.
>
> Food is a symbol of class there
> and cars are symbols of shoes.

People are symptoms of dreams.
Bombs are symptoms of rage.

Symbols—symptoms—no difference
in the leap to belligerence.

("O'CLOCK")

Note the ambiguity of reference: not a terrorized city but a "city of terror": a city that quite possibly breeds terror as much as it suffers from it. Note the civilians: marked only in their implicit opposition to soldiers. Note the "guys": are the guys the killed civilians or "they" who kill them? Regardless, the "guys" are both fathers and things, both humanized in their families and reified into the instruments or objects of death.

Here we have the exchange logic of belligerence, the equations of war: a symbolic logic, wholly operational. Marx reminds us that capitalist commodification aspires to turn the working person into a thing, a quantifiable unit whose labor power is one exchangeable commodity among the cars, food, files, sex, oil, and bombs humans are everywhere busily exchanging. In this poem it is as if Wordsworth had consorted with Marx and Dickinson to produce the fierce elegance of a lyric diagnosis. We see the violent thinginess of humans, a thinginess that Howe, like Wordsworth, alerts us to.

•

One comes to believe that prophecy is not a matter of telling the future but a practice of paying the strictest attention to the now. That what looks in Howe like a forecast fulfilled is in fact "the news" we get only from those poets committed to a kind of political and aesthetic attunement—the news we should get every day from poems, as William Carlos Williams hoped ("Asphodel, that greeny flower").

Long before the platitudes of globalization took shape, Howe was offering another kind of "Introduction to the World," as the title of one collection has it. A provisional world, hard in its limits but alterable; a world that calls forth a poetics of a rigorously uncertain register:

> This register is only a certainty
> If evolution's over and the created world
> Is done developing this place
> And its laws.
> ("INTRODUCTION TO THE WORLD")

This register is only a certainty *if*: *if* evolution's over. But of course the world is not done making itself, so the poet gives us a conditioned register, an ongoing interrogation.

Registered here is the awareness of the damage humans do as humans.

Herds of deer wander—their heads like wands
upraised for fear
of the human coming—and we always do.
(FROM "O'CLOCK")

We have brought a regime of terror to the animals, as well as to ourselves.

Yet

Even in wartime, there are objects
So suffused
With experience, that their pathos

Transforms them into something
As loving and potent as wine.
("ALSACE-LORRAINE")

Even in wartime one may see "an object of devotion / legitimate and romantic." Fanny Howe the dialectician, the romanticist and the satirist, the lacerator and the bringer of balm, the explorer of her and our contradictions: an American singer of the singular, contradictory song: "At least I know my tradition is among the contradictions." She has given you

—A rainbow
of emotions
("ALSACE-LORRAINE")

—the power of beauty

("ALSACE-LORRAINE")

—the ecstatic lash

("POEM FROM A SINGLE PALLET")

—A strap, something to hold onto . . .

(FROM "ALSACE-LORRAINE")

12

MY POETS I

AN INTERLUDE IN THE FORM OF A CENTO

I can hear little clicks inside my dream.[1]
This is a kind of thing that happens.[2]
There is, unfortunately, no test for truth.[3]
Does a firm perswasion that a thing is so, make it so?[4]
The new beginning inherent in birth makes itself felt in the
    world only because[5]
Experience is a hoax.[6]

Something hangs in back of me.[7]
Feelings: / oh, I have those; they / govern me,[8]

1. Anne Carson, "The Glass Essay."
2. Campbell McGrath, "The Bob Hope Poem."
3. Louise Glück, "Against Sincerity."
4. William Blake, *The Marriage of Heaven and Hell*.
5. Hannah Arendt, *The Human Condition*.
6. Alice Notley, "Experience."
7. Denise Levertov, "The Wings."
8. Glück, "The Red Poppy."

carve into me with knives of light.[9]

My genial spirits fail.[10]

Where shall I find a good sailor[11]

Like me, a believer in total immersion,[12]

If to the human mind's imaginings

Silence and solitude were vacancy?[13]

The ancient Poets animated all sensible objects with Gods or
   Geniuses.[14]

They are such fossils![15]

They relate differently to their autobiographical memories.[16]

They are alive and well somewhere.[17]

They are always watching with their little eyes, from my head
   to my feet.[18]

Rhyme, chime, echo, reiteration:[19]

there are believed to have been no casualties.[20]

9. Carson, "The Glass Essay."

10. Samuel Taylor Coleridge, "Dejection: An Ode."

11. Anonymous, "Sir Patrick Spens."

12. Elizabeth Bishop, "At the Fishhouses."

13. Percy Bysshe Shelley, "Mont Blanc."

14. Blake, *The Marriage of Heaven and Hell*.

15. McGrath, "The Bob Hope Poem."

16. Galen Strawson, "The Self and the SESMET."

17. Walt Whitman, "Song of Myself," section 6.

18. Whitman, "Song of Myself," canceled passage.

19. Denise Levertov, "Notes on Organic Form."

20. Bishop, "Twelve O'Clock News."

The limitless devaluation of everything given, this process of
    growing meaninglessness[21]
may look like (*Write* it!) like disaster.[22]
Give me hackneyed words because / they are good.[23]

This one's now for Judy.[24]
What dark thing have you done to me?[25]
Where are you off to, lady? for I see you[26]
Under an influence, swayed or swaying.[27]
O Lady! we receive but what we give.[28]
We love each other like we grew / from the same set of pelvic
    bone[29]
And so the old antinomies of "I" and "the other," of the
    individual and society, fall.[30]

21. Arendt, *The Human Condition.*
22. Bishop, "One Art."
23. Lisa Robertson, *The Weather.*
24. Robertson, *The Weather.*
25. Rachel Zucker, *Museum of Accidents.*
26. Whitman, "Song of Myself," section 11.
27. Bernadette Mayer, "The Obfuscated Poem."
28. Coleridge, "Dejection: An Ode."
29. Lucie Brock-Broido, "Elective Mutes."
30. Emile Benveniste, "Subjectivity in Language."

I decided to take on the self.[31]
That's why I read, as a stranger,[32]
and cry out, my love, each to each[33]
and then my heart with pleasure fills.[34]

Everything becomes clear when one recognizes *avoir* for what
    it is.[35]
Go make you ready.[36]
C'mon and show me something newer than even Dante.[37]
I can't get him out of my mind, out of my mind,[38]
geometric, deformed, unnatural.[39]
If he had a sense of identity it was probably with a stone.[40]

31. Strawson, "The Self and the SESMET."

32. Fernando Pessoa, "I don't know how many souls I have," trans.
Richard Zenith.

33. Paul Muldoon, "The Grand Conversation."

34. Wordsworth, "I Wandered Lonely as a Cloud."

35. Benveniste, "Functions of 'To Be' and 'To Have.'"

36. Frank Bidart, "Advice to the Players."

37. Mayer, "Sonnet."

38. John Berryman, "Dream Song 155."

39. Elizabeth Alexander, "The Venus Hottentot."

40. Zbigniew Herbert, "Sense of Identity," trans. John and Bogdana
Carpenter.

On the brink of a potentially bathetic melodrama,[41]
The great thing / is not having / a mind.[42]

We want to speak the beautiful language of our times.[43]
All the bells say: too late. This is not for tears;[44]
"i" thinks "i live more in a continuous present that i enjoy."[45]
One's nakedness is very slow.[46]
We may yet construct our future[47]
dark, salt, clear, moving, utterly free.[48]
How the invisible / roils.[49]

My purpose here is to advance into / the sense of the weather.[50]
In the next millennium I will be middle aged.[51]
I speak / because I am shattered,[52]

41. Carson, "The Glass Essay."

42. Glück, "The Red Poppy."

43. Robertson, *The Weather.*

44. Berryman, "Dream Song 29."

45. Olena Kalytiak Davis, "The Lyric 'I' Drives to Pick Up Her Children from School: A Poem in the Postconfessional Mode."

46. Jorie Graham, "Evolution."

47. Muldoon, "The Grand Conversation."

48. Bishop, "At the Fishhouses."

49. Graham, "Notes on the Reality of the Self."

50. Robertson, *The Weather.*

51. Brock-Broido, "Domestic Mysticism."

52. Glück, "The Red Poppy."

hung-over / after a wedding party row[53]
a resurrection weed inside of me[54]
& all of England at my beckoned call.[55]

Listen, I was not saying anything.[56]
I hear, I hear, with joy I hear![57]

It's new for me / to be hearing cicadas.[58]
Cicadas exist, chicory, chromium / and chrome yellow
    irises.[59]
My fellow citizen cicadas rise to the tops of the vanished Twin
    Towers.[60]

I cling like a cicada to the latticework of memory,[61]
the transformation of the actual to the true.[62]

53. Tom Pickard, "Driving to Killhope."
54. Brock-Broido, "Elective Mutes."
55. Brock-Broido, "Edward VI on the Seventh Day."
56. Graham, "Prayer."
57. Wordsworth, "Ode: Intimations of Immortality."
58. Inger Christensen, *Alphabet*.
59. Christensen, *Alphabet*.
60. Frederick Seidel, "The Bush Administration."
61. Henri Cole, "Self-Portrait in a Gold Kimono."
62. Glück, "Against Sincerity."

I could not choose words. I am free to go.[63]

I wonder what kind of Liberty this is.[64]

Sometimes, at night, I wish I'd married Norman.[65]

63. Graham, "Prayer."
64. Carson, "The Glass Essay."
65. Zucker, *Museum of Accidents*.

13

MY EMILY DICKINSON/
MY EMILY DICKINSON

Emily Dickinson: post-9/11 poet?

I began to consider this question after returning to Susan Howe's *My Emily Dickinson*, her kaleidoscopic, deeply researched, brilliantly written 1985 tour de force, which was reissued in 2007 with a new introduction by Eliot Weinberger.

Weinberger calls *My Emily Dickinson* a "classic" of "avantgardist criticism," and he invokes a lineage of poets' criticism extending from William Carlos Williams (*In the American Grain*) to Charles Olson (*Call Me Ishmael*) to "Susan Howe herself, the most Americanist of American poets."

Howe's book is simultaneously a dazzling exploration of Dickinson's power and an anatomy of the American cultural imaginary. "The vivid rhetoric of terror," Howe writes, "was a first step in the slow process of American Democracy." This rhetoric of terror—fueled by a double legacy of Calvinist predestinarianism and violent frontier experience—animates some of Dickinson's best work.

It seemed to me that alongside Auden's "September 1, 1939," much circulated in the weeks after September 11, one might do equally well to return to a homegrown poet of terror, abjection, and difficulty:

> What Terror would enthrall the Street
> Could Countenance disclose
>
> The Subterranean Freight
> The Cellars of the Soul—
>
> (1211)

> Dust is the only Secret—
> Death, the only One
> You cannot find out all about
> In his "native town"
>
> (166)

> One Anguish—in a Crowd—
> A Minor thing—it sounds—
> And yet, unto the single Doe
> Attempted—of the Hounds

> 'Tis Terror as consummate
> As Legions of Alarm
> Did leap . . .
>
> (527)

Terror as perspectival experience. A "War on Terror" neces-
sarily lodges itself within. Duct Tape. Code Red. Enriched
Uranium. We are called to feel a general, perhaps fraudulent,
fright, an ecstasy of alertness:

> It sets the Fright at liberty—
> And Terror's free—
> Gay, Ghastly, Holiday!
>
> (341)

A focal point of Howe's book is an extended examination of
"My Life had stood—a Loaded Gun—," a poem that, after
Howe's exhaustive, inventive scrutiny, you will hear as inter-
nalizing a vast poetic tradition as well as a profound con-
sciousness of historical trauma. "This is a frontier poem,"
Howe asserts. Dickinson becomes both pioneer and weapon,
maker and instrument.

Howe writes: " 'My Life had stood—a Loaded Gun—' (764) ex-
plores the ambiguous terrain of dream, between power and
execution, sensuality and sadism—here the poet would tread
and draw blood. Trigger-happy with false meaning her poem
is an ambiguity of progress, a descant on dissembling."

To foe of His—I'm deadly foe—

None stir the second time—

(764)

How to reply to a shot? With a shot?

Howe gives us a Dickinson passionately reading, hearing, and counterhearing. She undertakes for Dickinson what she calls an "archaeology." In a series of bravura readings, Howe evokes a complex heritage of captivity narratives, frontier experience, King Philip's War (1675–76), the ideas of the Puritan ministers Cotton and Increase Mather, and antinomian dissidence alongside Dickinson's intense engagement with Shakespeare, Browning, George Eliot, the Brontës.

It is striking that in Susan Faludi's book *The Terror Dream: Fear and Fantasy in Post-9/11 America* (2007), she invokes a similar inheritance or template—a "phylogeny," in her metaphor. Captivity narratives, frontier tropes, Calvinist fear and trembling, the annihilating violence of wars against the Indians— these inform Faludi's analysis of our current cultural horizon just as they inform Howe's *My Emily Dickinson*. Mary Rowlandson's bestselling seventeenth-century captivity narrative, Hannah Dustin's 1697 captivity and violent self-organized escape, the legend of Daniel Boone: for Faludi—as for Howe— these become crucial sites for exploring the ambiguities of

American (self-)mythologizing. Thus Faludi analyzes the dynamics of "Saving Jessica Lynch." Better to have a story about straight-up masculine rescue, about imperiled and possibly raped damsels stage-liberated for cameras, than a messy account of injured soldiers, both male and female, cared for by Iraqi doctors. Captivity narratives—whether from Puritan writers or broadcast on TV—supposedly reauthorize patriarchal authority (God's, the husband's, the American army's) in their accounts of trial and deliverance. Yet in Faludi's telling, these stories also reveal the profound anxiety provoked by the specter of male failure and defenselessness, of women with agency, of women themselves willing to use violence (Hannah Dustin slew her Indian captors and, after escaping, returned to scalp them).

In Faludi's book, King Philip's War is only one episode in a long history of America's terror fixation, a dread of and longing for destruction. The witchcraft trials are another such episode. Dickinson:

> What Terror would enthrall the Street
> Could Countenance disclose
>
> The Subterranean Freight
> The Cellars of the Soul—
>
> (1211)

Sinners in the hands of an angry god. Apostate communities subjected to trials and tribulations. "We have insulted God at the highest level of our government. Then, we say 'why does this happen?' It is happening because God Almighty is lifting His protection from us" (Pat Robertson). Or, and: Blowback. Boomerang. *Why do they hate us?* Unintended consequences. Unknown unknowns.

Every country has its origin myths, even if its myth is that it has no origin. A people under attack will ramp up its mythmaking and myth-preserving energies. So it was during King Philip's War in the late seventeenth century, and so it has been these past several years, as Faludi argues throughout *The Terror Dream*.

The Truth, is Bald—and Cold—

(341)

One thinks of the failure of representation since 9/11, the proliferation of novels, the media glut, the surfeit of images that somehow slide too easily into a banal repertoire, commodified shock. Here Dickinson's ceaseless instinct for negation, distinction, refinement, annihilation, seems wholly relevant, when things are

... most, like Chaos—Stopless—cool—
Without a Chance, or spar—

Or even a Report of Land—
To justify—Despair.

(355)

Her lines can seem uncannily, New Englandly, to anticipate some of the more controversial responses to 9/11. For example, Karlheinz Stockhausen's infamous (and, when read in full, complex) meditation on the destruction of that day as infernal art, aesthetic cataclysm:

'Tis so appalling—it exhilirates—
So over Horror, it half captivates—

(341)

Or Susan Sontag's dissenting remarks published in *The New Yorker*, September 24, 2001—

The disconnect between last Tuesday's monstrous dose of reality and the self-righteous drivel and outright deceptions being peddled by public figures and TV commentators is startling, depressing. The voices licensed to follow the event seem to have joined together in a campaign to infantilize the public. Where is the acknowledgment that this was not a "cowardly" attack on "civilization" or "liberty" or "humanity" or "the free world" but an attack on the world's self-proclaimed superpower, undertaken as a consequence of specific American alliances and actions?

—remarks that launched—as Faludi reminds us—an ecstasy of righteous denunciation. Per Dickinson:

> Assent—and you are sane—
> Demur—you're straightway dangerous—
> And handled with a Chain—
>
> (620)

So, too, the politics of memorializing Ground Zero might have been chastened by Dickinson's astringency:

> After a hundred years
> Nobody knows the Place
> Agony that enacted there
> Motionless as Peace
>
> (1149)

It is perhaps tiresome to return to these episodes, this ritualized, reified, inane diction of outrage and stasis, which for some time it seemed Barack Obama's change machine might fully challenge. One could hope.

But one can also think. And this is what Dickinson arouses us to do, and what Howe on Dickinson challenges us to do: "Is Awe Nature; and destruction the beginning of every Foundation? Do words flee their meaning? Define definition."

•

Sometime late in 2001 or early in 2002, I was in New York City and heard Susan Howe give a talk at the Drawing Center in SoHo (I think). There she spoke about flags, about Whitman's pennant, about Melville's, about her memories of being prohibited access to university libraries, about "official" exhibits of history (e.g., at Harvard's Widener Library) versus rigorous, dialectical accounts. On that evening, and long after, and still at times, this most Americanist of American poets was the only one, it seemed, who had anything to say worth listening to. "Forcing, abbreviating, pushing, padding, subtracting, riddling, interrogating, re-writing, she pulled text from text." Howe on Dickinson, applicable to Howe herself.

In *My Emily Dickinson*, Howe reports the following: "In her letter to Mabel Todd, the fifty-five-year-old Emily Dickinson quoted Emerson and signed herself 'America.'"

In that letter of summer 1885, Dickinson wrote:

> "Sweet Land of Liberty" is a superfluous Carol till it concern ourselves—then it outrealms the Birds.
> I saw the American Flag last Night in the shutting West, and I felt for every Exile.

I like to think of Emily Dickinson being read in other countries. Is she so provincial that she will not travel? Her metaphysic is mobile; "The Brain—is wider than the Sky—." She seems ever primed for the strange, possibly annihilating encounter. She presents herself, mock-ingenuously, as transmitting

> The simple News that Nature told—
> With tender Majesty
>
> Her message is committed
> To Hands I cannot see—
> For love of Her—Sweet—countrymen—
> Judge tenderly—of Me
>
> (519)

I used to think those lines encoded a double appeal: that they asked us, her "Sweet—countrymen" and -women, to judge tenderly of Dickinson, because of our regard for "Her," that is, Nature; and/or that they asked us, future readers, countrymen or not, to judge Emily Dickinson tenderly "for love" of her sweet surrounding contemporaries. These lines call for a kind of compassion, a historical humility: Be kind to me, countrymen, and take me as one who aspired to transmit the message of "Nature." Yet also: Be kind not only to me, but to us, to those who lived before.

These lines read to me now as an additional appeal, another kind of leap into an unknown futurity. Emily Dickinson's messages are committed to hands I cannot see, hands elsewhere on this earth, or in the future; whether those unknown people to whom her message might be committed will judge her by her countrymen, whether if they do so they will be inclined thereby to judge "tenderly" of her, I cannot say. Some—both our countrymen, and those devoted to destroying our countrymen—will continue to do as George Oppen wrote in "Of Being Numerous":

> They carry nativeness
> To a conclusion
> In suicide.

But "This World is not conclusion" (373). We are not done with Dickinson, nor she with us. "A something overtakes the mind —we do not hear it coming," Dickinson wrote. Yet, once it has come, the mind recovers or collapses or deforms, meeting what has come and what may yet come in better or worse ways. Faludi challenges us "to imagine a national identity grounded not on virile illusion but on the talents and vitality of all of us equally, men and women both." Dickinson proposes a Nation within—

> One—is the Population—
> Numerous enough—
> This ecstatic Nation
> Seek—it is Yourself.

> (1381)

—and imagines the irrepressible, insurgent heart outflanking the police:

> The mob within the heart
> Police cannot suppress
> The riot given at the first
> Is authorized as peace
>
> (1763)

Perhaps it is merely a higher, typically American narcissism to see in the events of 9/11 and their aftermath "opportunities," as Faludi puts it, "to look at ourselves anew." Yet Dickinson's question hangs suspended, a perpetual address: "How is it Hearts, with Thee?" (175).

14

MY SHELLEY/
(MY ROMANTICS)

For let us praise Shelley.

For Shelley may need a defense.

So let us dispraise Shelley.

For a *Defence of Poetry* may both praise and blame.

For the difference between *defense* and *defence* is one difference between America and England.

For a *Defence of Poetry* need not entail a *Defence of Shelley* but Shelley's *Defence* yet has legs.

For Shelley is immortal his embers ever fading ever glowing coals to warm your heart by.

For Shelley is mortal his embers ever fading his body burnt in the bonfire on the shore his pale thin body drowned his hot heart retrieved from the ashes by Edward Trelawny and kept ever after by Mary Shelley.

For my Shelley is a portal to the infinite we've put paid to laying our heads on the grave of the possible.

•

O Shelley O contradiction O skylark bird thou never wert!

An Oxford don, one A.O.J. Cockshut, best known to the world for his work on Anthony Trollope and Walter Scott and to students for his zealous Catholicism, this Mr. Cockshut was one day in 1990 brought to exclaim: The idiocy! Of course that skylark was a bird!

Here we confront, and not for the last time, one limit of English criticism.

Shelley!—Mary Godwin cried out on the staircase and on her mother's tombstone in the Old St Pancras Churchyard braced against it there ecstatic while they fucked. Shelley!

Though most likely they did not use the diction of fucking as they were high-minded and delicate and soul-pledging and wished to protect their love and their sex from mere vulgarity.
Though a dash of vulgarity might have usefully leavened Shelley's ethereal bread and let Mary know what was in store.
For despite his freeloving atheistical radical reputation Shelley had a good streak of the Puritan about him. Let us not forget that Puritans were true radicals.

•

For Shelley had an abhorrence of the low.
And of cynicism; of easy irony; of the cheap.
Byron enthralled and depressed him.

For regarding Shelley in all his blazing complexity one might consult the exhilarating and still unobsolete *Shelley: The Pursuit*, by Richard Holmes.

And Daisy Hay's *Young Romantics: The Shelleys, Byron, and Other Tangled Lives* is of interest. And see especially Ann Wroe, *Being Shelley*.

But again: Shelley!

For a Gothic ecstasy is not to be gainsaid.

For teenagers have sex and they like it.

For Romeo and Juliet are paradigms.

For everyone knows this and envies the youth of the world their liberties when they take them and their brief bloom.

•

For Larkin: *sexual intercourse began / In nineteen sixty-three / (which was rather late for me).*

For Wordsworth: *Bliss was it in that dawn to be alive / But to be young was very heaven!*

For this was so for both girls and boys, but soon was less so for girls.

For sexed bodies are not equivalent and the world bears harder on those who bear children.

For while the rectum may be a grave in the era of AIDS (to invoke Leo Bersani) the vagina has been a grave for millennia.

Viz. Mary Wollstonecraft dead of infection some ten days after giving birth to Mary Godwin.

For thus the fear of sex a wholly reasonable fear and it is a fear that has been borne largely by females.

Dead babies and dead mothers and dead babies and ghosts and hosts of heavens populated by dead poets and dead poets' babies insufficiently tended or abandoned or lost. Clara William Allegra.

●

It is easy to imagine Byron having sex indeed we have his ample testimony of fucking wide and low and near and far as he said of his own *Don Juan*

> is it not *life*, is it not *the thing*?—Could any man have written
> it—who has not lived in the world?—who has not tooled in
> a post-chaise? in a hackney coach? in a gondola? against a
> wall? in a court carriage?—in a vis a vis?—on a table?—and
> under it?

(LETTER, BYRON TO DOUGLAS KINNAIRD, OCTOBER 26, 1819)

Yes Byron was *Mad Bad and Dangerous to Know* he rogers his half sister he abuses his wife he carouses with boys he out-Satans Satan he liberates Greece in his mind and he fights there while Shelley was *Mad Glad and Dangerous to Know* he abandons his first wife he romances Mary Godwin's stepsister he careers around London avoiding his debtors he generates an angelology of love he liberates Greece in his mind; Shelley mad to commonsense Englishmen; to his upright father; glad in spirits; gladdening friends and some lovers; dangerous to himself at times, to servants enmeshed in his schemes; dangerous to women, to Harriet the pretty first wife discarded for Mary Godwin, Harriet self-drowned in the Serpentine.

Is it not *life*?
Is it not *the thing*?

Then, what is life? I cried—
(SHELLEY, "THE TRIUMPH OF LIFE")

• • • •

In Shelley, with Shelley, we encounter the peril of the idealist. A peril for those more or differently embodied. And differently classed.

Of his metaphysically inflected poetry, Mary Shelley observed, "He loved to idealize reality; and this is a taste shared by few."

In almost the last thing she wrote about Shelley, Harriet called him "a vampire."

William Hazlitt said of Thomas Robert Malthus: "He turns the world into a charnel-house."

Shelley used that very imagery in his more Gothic poems, as when in "Alastor; or, The Spirit of Solitude" he addresses the "Mother of this unfathomable world!":

> I have made my bed
> In charnels and on coffins, where black death
> Keeps record of the trophies won from thee,
> Hoping to still these obstinate questionings
> Of thee and thine, by forcing some lone ghost,
> Thy messenger, to render up the tale
> Of what we are.
>
> ("ALASTOR," LL. 23–29)

One can't but note how close is the charnel to the "deep Mother"; one notes as well the speaker's simultaneously adversarial and adulatory relation to her.

In Shelley's last unfinished poem, "The Triumph of Life,"
his interlocutor Rousseau offers an infernal vision of the pow-
erful "who make this earth their charnel" (l. 505).

Mary Shelley invokes horrific charnel-house muckings-
about in *Frankenstein*, the monster made in part from dead
bits Victor Frankenstein's collected.

Is the world a charnel house?

Cf. the monsters.

Cf. the dead babies.

And the mothers.

● ● ● ●

Shelley! You should be living at this hour—

Shelley! Perhaps you are or were alive again amid the head-
long youth of the sixties rising O Shelley I saw you there you
were a soixante-huitard!

For *ROUSE UP, O YOUNG MEN of the new age! Set your fore-
heads against the ignorant Hirelings!*

For

>   Men of England, wherefore plough
>   For the lords who lay ye low?
>   Wherefore weave with toil and care
>   The rich robes your tyrants wear?
>   **("SONG TO THE MEN OF ENGLAND")**

For you did not cease from mental fight!
For yet we still cannot say

> The loathsome mask has fallen, the man remains
> Sceptreless, free, uncircumscribed—but man:
> Equal, unclassed, tribeless and nationless,
> Exempt from awe, worship, degree . . .
> (*PROMETHEUS UNBOUND*, III.IV.193–96)

The loathsome mask has not yet fallen.
For Shelley death is not dead.
And you are *To thy high requiem become a sod.*
The hungry generations tread thee down.
Shelley!

> Turn thee, surpassing Spirit!
> Much yet remains unscanned.
> (*QUEEN MAB*, III.14–15)

● ● ● ●

For when I was reading him I approached the incandescent
 youth with some ideas and a motif, an idea of immortality
 and an idea of revolution and a musical motif—

For he is with Keats the great musician of English verse—and,
 in the mordant words of Theodor Adorno, these two poets

might be seen as the "*locum tenentes* of nonexistent great English composers" (*Introduction to the Sociology of Music*).

And unlike Keats, Shelley does not lapse so regularly into the cloying—though he too can cloy and can annoy: viz. "I fall upon the thorns of life! I bleed!" ("Ode to the West Wind," l. 54); viz. certain unfortunate passages in "Epipsychidion."

For you can judge a man in part by his enemies.
And with friends like Matthew Arnold, Shelley didn't need enemies.
But among his later enemies were Eliot and Pound.
And Shelley was loathed by many of his contemporaries; even politically sympathetic men like John Keats and William Hazlitt "cordially disliked" Shelley as Richard Holmes notes for his blithe aristocratic hauteur.
But Browning, Yeats, and Ginsberg cherished him and rightly—

For no major romantic inspires such irritation as Shelley—viz. T. S. Eliot:

The ideas of Shelley seem to me always to be the ideas of adolescence—as there is every reason why they should be. And an enthusiasm for Shelley seems to me also to be an affair of adolescence.

And:

> But some of Shelley's views I positively dislike, and that
> hampers my enjoyment of the poems in which they occur;
> and others seem to me so puerile that I cannot enjoy the po-
> ems in which they occur.

("SHELLEY AND KEATS," IN THE USE OF
POETRY AND THE USE OF CRITICISM)

This is worth pondering.

Many famous Romantic poets died early and left beautiful
and/or ravaged corpses.

And even if they lived long lives, the poets of this period did
seem to show a particular interest in childhood, adolescence,
and theories of development. The Child is father of the Man,
etc.

Keats forthrightly and touchingly apologizes for the imma-
turity of *Endymion* in his preface:

> Knowing within myself the manner in which this Poem has
> been produced, it is not without a feeling of regret that I
> make it public.
>
> What manner I mean, will be quite clear to the reader,
> who must soon perceive great inexperience, immaturity,
> and every error denoting a feverish attempt, rather than a
> deed accomplished.

Such a preface might be regarded as a preemptive strike.

The poet-prodigy and forger Thomas Chatterton, dead at seventeen, was something like the Kurt Cobain of his era. His suicide in 1770 sent ripples of sympathetic identification through all fellow poets for more than fifty years. Keats's *Endymion* is "inscribed to the memory of Thomas Chatterton, 1818." He was *that marvelous boy* (Wordsworth). He was that remembered, honored, sacrificed adolescent. Shelley salutes Chatterton in "Adonais," his elegy for Keats: "Chatterton / Rose pale, his solemn agony had not / Yet faded from him . . ."

One feels that there must be options other than a perpetually stalled adolescence (as Eliot views Shelley's condition) and a neurotically overasserted maturity (as one might gloss Eliot's).

In years to come Mary Shelley would look back at her youth, and Shelley's, with a chastened, judicious eye: "It is seldom that the young know what youth is, till they have got beyond its period; and time was not given to him to attain this knowledge" (preface to the *Poetical Works*, 1939).

For "He had been from youth the victim of the state of feeling inspired by the reaction of the French Revolution."

And "He looked on political freedom as the direct agent to effect the happiness of mankind; and thus any new-sprung hope of liberty inspired a joy and an exultation more intense and wild than he could have felt for any personal advantage."

For with Shelley *the political is personal.*

•

For yet one might also recall César Vallejo: *Los intelectuales son rebeldes, pero no revolucionarios.*

For given Shelley's violent estrangement from his father, his careering from one radical cause to another, his impetuous antiauthoritarianism, one might say that he was tremendously Oedipalized, a case of "oppositional defiance."

Yet Shelley will forever elude the strictures of the *Diagnostic and Statistical Manual of Mental Disorders.*

● ● ● ●

When I was young I never felt young I felt oppressed constrained at times naive suffused with earnestness and inchoate high thoughts all of which is to say that I was young and a certain type of young person though I did not feel young and I resented anyone who said "ah but you are young." And I resent them still.

Though when an openhearted one says *I feel young* or *That is what youth meant* she means the openhanded joy of Blake's *Glad Day* she means

> *Bliss was it in that dawn to be alive*

she means

We have passed Age's icy caves

she means

My soul is an Enchanted boat

she means

Exuberance is Beauty

though for many years this kind of rising spirit did not touch
me or rather it touched me quick but as a scalpel probes the
wound—
for I lived in no medium sustaining of an ever-fleeting joy.
And what of happiness?

> It seems to float ever—forever—
> Upon that many-winding River,
> Between mountains, woods, abysses,
> A paradise of wildernesses!
> **(PROMETHEUS UNBOUND, II.V.78–81)**

Shelley was, as Mary Shelley wrote, passionately "attached
to the cause of human happiness and improvement."
He was endlessly envisioning "a nation / Made free by love"
(*The Revolt of Islam*, 1839–40).
Of his *Revolt of Islam*, he declared in his preface: "There is
no quarter given to Revenge, or Envy, or prejudice. Love is cel-

ebrated everywhere as the sole law which should govern the moral world."

Yet what is love?

• • • •

If I say "revolution" you might think America or France or Russia or if you were a certain kind of historian you might think "Glorious" or if another kind "sexual" or "Cultural" or "permanent."

Shelley was born at the tail end of the French Revolution, "the most astonishing thing that has hitherto happened in the world" in Edmund Burke's words; and he lived fanning its embers wherever he saw their still-glowing light—publishing an atheistical tract while at Oxford; campaigning for Catholic Emancipation while in Ireland; agitating for free love and vegetarianism; seeking out the great anarchist and theorist of nonviolent revolution, William Godwin, whose *Political Justice* came out in 1793, the year after Shelley's birth, and whose lover and briefly wife was Mary Wollstonecraft—another of Shelley's heroes.

Indeed Shelley dedicated *The Revolt of Islam* "To Mary——," his lover then wife Mary Godwin, in stanzas saluting her famous progenitors, Mary Wollstonecraft and William Godwin:

XII

They say that thou wert lovely from thy birth,
  Of glorious parents, thou aspiring Child.
I wonder not—for One then left this earth
  Whose life was like a setting planet mild,
  Which clothed thee in the radiance undefiled
Of its departing glory; still her fame
  Shines on thee, through the tempests dark and wild
Which shake these latter days; and thou canst claim
The shelter, from thy Sire, of an immortal name.

(LL. 100–108)

O feminism o grave thing!
Her fame / Shines on thee.
Can man be free if woman be a slave? (*The Revolt of Islam*, l. 1045).
Shelley:

> Let this opportunity be conceded to me of acknowledging
> that I have, what a Scotch philosopher characteristically
> terms, "a passion for reforming the world:" what passion in-
> cited him to write and publish his book, he omits to explain.
> For my part I had rather be damned with Plato and Lord Ba-
> con, than go to Heaven with Paley and Malthus. But it is a
> mistake to suppose that I dedicate my poetical composi-
> tions solely to the direct enforcement of reform, or that I

consider them in any degree as containing a reasoned system on the theory of human life.

(PREFACE TO *PROMETHEUS UNBOUND*)

Shelley with his *passion for reforming the world*—
yet as Bernadette Mayer insists in "The Obfuscated Poem":
"Poetry's not a business; it was not her business or his to remake the world."

Yet even Wordsworth conceded, reflecting on his time in France during the Revolution:

> Yet would I willingly have taken up
> A service at this time for cause so great,
> However dangerous . . .

(*THE PRELUDE*, BOOK X, RESIDENCE IN FRANCE, 134–36)

And when a sobered person reflects on everything that was and seemed about to be she may cry, as Wordsworth did:

> Whither is fled the visionary gleam?
> Where is it now, the glory and the dream?

("ODE: INTIMATIONS OF IMMORTALITY")

And Shelley later echoed:

> Whither have fled
> The hues of heaven that canopied his bower
> Of yesternight? . . .

("ALASTOR," LL. 196–98)

And she may wonder

> Whence are we, and why are we? of what scene
> The actors or spectators? . . .
>
> ("ADONAIS," LL. 184–85)

When one considers the failure of the French Revolution, the dreams borne therein, the vicious reaction of established state and religious powers in Britain and on the Continent; when one considers the smashing of the Commune; when one considers the repeated extinguishing of inflamed hopes, one might conclude, following Coleridge: *My genial spirits fail* ("Dejection: An Ode," l. 39).

Ah one might say (as Louise Glück does in a poem in *The Wild Iris* imagining her son's rebuke to her miserablism): "Typical depressive."

And as Hannah Arendt argued in *On Revolution*, dreams of revolutionary happiness are in the end religious, not political, dreams.

And certainly Shelley was keen to fuse psychological and sexual with political aspirations; and he was insufficiently mindful that political commitments might well channel non- or prepolitical needs.

And like Arendt herself he made a distinction between the American and French Revolutions: in *A Philosophical View of Reform* Shelley refers to the "just and successful Revolt of America" in contradistinction to the "French Revolution."

And it is not at all clear that the French Revolution did not succeed, and brilliantly—for as a sage Chinese is reported to have said, it is still too early to tell.

Still, as Mary Shelley wrote in her "Note on *Prometheus Unbound*," "Shelley believed that mankind had only to will that there should be no evil, and there would be none . . . That man could be so perfectionized as to be able to expel evil from his own nature, and from the greater part of the creation, was the cardinal point of his system."

Shelley lacked a theory of political violence. He did not believe in *the death drive*. Or *the aggressive instinct*. Or original sin.

Like William Godwin, whose *Political Justice* fortified him in this doctrine, he believed in *the perfectibility of man*.

Hogwash! said Edmund Burke; said Thomas Robert Malthus; said Hannah Arendt.

And they are not wrong.

Yet—

• • • •

What do we want from our poets?

From this poet?

Language pressured into inevitability and permanence?

Consciousness shaped into a laser of insight?

Poetry's not a business; it was not her business or his to remake the world.

> Mr. Forester.
>
> What then becomes of the hopes of the world, which you have admitted to consist entirely in the progress of the mind, allowing, as you must allow, the incontrovertible fact of the physical deterioration of the human race?
>
> Mr. Fax.
>
> When I speak of the mind, I do not allude either to poetry or to periodical criticism, nor in any great degree to physical science; but I rest my hopes on the very same basis with Mr. Mystic's fear—the general diffusion of moral and political truth.
>
> Mr. Forester.
>
> For poetry, its best days are gone . . .
>
> (THOMAS LOVE PEACOCK, *MELINCOURT*)

So says the Shelleyan Mr. Forester to the Malthusian Mr. Fax in *Melincourt*, Thomas Love Peacock's satirical novel of ideas: *For poetry, its best days are gone.*

And this may be so.

For *nowadays the talent goes elsewhere.*

For why poetry when movies and video games and YouTube and Facebook and pop and porn.

For yet Anne Carson's "Glass Essay," her *Autobiography of Red*; for yet Christian Bök's *Eunoia*; for Inger Christensen's *Alphabet* and *It*; for Joshua Clover's *The Totality for Kids*; for Claudia Rankine's *Don't Let Me Be Lonely*; for Rachel

Zucker's *Museum of Accidents*. For August Kleinzahler Frank Bidart Devin Johnston Lisa Robertson Tom Pickard Durs Grünbein Susan Stewart Frederick Seidel Katie Peterson Ciaran Carson Alane Rollings Elizabeth Arnold Ed Barrett Harryette Mullen Paul Muldoon Cathy Park Hong Olena Kalytiak Davis Eleni Sikelianos Roy Fisher.

• • • •

For Shelley is anthologized: thus I first met him, hymning Intellectual Beauty, subliming Mont Blanc, blown by the west wind toward a spring he could not but question.

For Shelley is a great questioner—ceaseless questioner—asking of Mont Blanc:

> And what were thou, and earth, and stars, and sea,
> If to the human mind's imaginings
> Silence and solitude were vacancy?

("MONT BLANC," LL. 142–44)

Addressing "Intellectual Beauty":

> I vowed that I would dedicate my powers
> To thee and thine—have I not kept the vow?

("HYMN TO INTELLECTUAL BEAUTY," LL. 61–62)

Questioning the West Wind:

If Winter comes, can Spring be far behind?

("ODE TO THE WEST WIND," L. 70)

If he is best known for shorter lyrics, his full power is not then felt, for there is a shining architecture in such mythopoeic works as *Prometheus Unbound*, a propulsive inward critical immolation in the earlier journey-poem "Alastor"—one of the best examples of what Harold Bloom called "the internalization of quest romance." He is at times esoteric, he is complex, his poems playing out on a mental theater often far from the sturdy *rocks, and stones, and trees* of Wordsworth, and seemingly alien to the pithy compact diabolical glimmerings of Blake's songs. Like Blake, he had a mythy mind. Unlike Blake he did not strive to *create his own system or be enslaved by another man's.* He reanimated what he felt was the spirit of Greece—of liberty, of music, of body, of thought. He'd studied Hume, Locke, Plato, and was no superficial student. He called his early work *Queen Mab* "a philosophic poem," and he was right. To immerse yourself in him is to move through an extraordinary medium of thinking songs, sung thoughts. And if *an enthusiasm for Shelley seems to me also to be an affair of adolescence,* let us not prematurely renounce the searching passions we contain and often denigrate in the term "adolescent." For as Adam Phillips observes, "the adolescent is somebody who is trying to escape from a cult."

•

I had no imagination so I sought out the imaginers:

Poetry, in a general sense, may be defined to be "the expression of the Imagination": and poetry is connate with the origin of man.

(SHELLEY, "A DEFENCE OF POETRY")

Imagination! lifting up itself
Before the eye and progress of my song . . .

(WORDSWORTH, THE PRELUDE, VI.525–26)

To whom then am I addressed? To the imagination.

(WILLIAMS, *SPRING AND ALL*)

To refine, to clarify, to intensify that eternal moment in which we alone live there is but a single force—the imagination.

(WILLIAMS, *SPRING AND ALL*)

One aspect of Shelley is too little acknowledged: the counterfactual imagination. He strenuously redoes the French Revolution precisely to examine its failure in *The Revolt of Islam*; he pitches the liberation of Man and Mind in another, optative key in *Prometheus Unbound*; the outbreak of the War of Greek Independence in 1821 provoked him to launch another revolutionary drama, *Hellas*. He ceaselessly inquires into the what if, yet always cleaves to the undone, paying his debt to the pressure of the negative. A true dialectician, he does not

bypass the phase of negation required for any higher synthe-
sis: thus the astonishing proliferation of kinetic negatives
throughout his work, even at the level of diction:

Viz. the "unrelaxing speed" of the poet's boat in "Alastor"
(l. 366).

And the "unresting sound" of the torrent of the river Arve
in "Mont Blanc" (l. 33).

And the mind's "unremitting interchange / With the clear
universe of things around" in "Mont Blanc" (ll. 39–40).

And the vision of Man in *Prometheus Unbound*:

> Sceptreless, free, uncircumscribed—but man:
> Equal, unclassed, tribeless and nationless . . .
>
> (III.IV.194–95)

● ● ● ●

Romantic poets are often disoriented.
They are often struggling to orient themselves.

> I was lost as in a cloud,
> Halted, without a struggle to break through.
>
> (WORDSWORTH, *THE PRELUDE*, VI.529–30)

When I was returned from England to the United States bro-
ken and frayed I turned around every time I heard someone
on the street with an American accent. Which is to say I was
always turning around.

I had not adjusted to the acoustic shift, this move from what
had been "marked," as the linguists say (American accents
heard in Oxford), to the "unmarked" (American accents
heard in America).

I could not say *I hear, I hear, with joy I hear!* (Wordsworth, "Ode:
Intimations of Immortality," l. 51).

For though *Joy is the sweet voice, Joy the luminous cloud* (Co-
leridge, "Dejection: An Ode," l. 71), *I was lost as in a cloud.*

For I did not hear her.

My ears were still tuned elsewhere.

And my eyes saw what they would—

And for months I would think I saw her on the street and time
and again I nearly cried out: O!

O Love!

But of course I was not seeing her, who was over three thou-
sand miles away.

I forgot / That I had bodily eyes (Wordsworth, *The Prelude*,
ll. 368–69).

I was in a sense hallucinating.

Shelley hallucinated ghosts—or, we could say, he saw them.

The empirically absent are often more present than the body
before you, or in you.

There is a body in language and a body in the language.

When I was with a new lover I was stunned once to find myself
crying out the name of my ex-husband.

I was brought again to learn how one might be haunted.

I was not thinking at all about him; I was not thinking. I was moving and was moved and thus the voice utters *the other name*. The throat a strange conduit. *Song of the bleeding throat*, as Whitman says. It lingered in the air almost swallowed.

One could attribute this to a conditioned reflex or to some complex stimulus-response effect. One could.

One reaches backward and forward through a sound. A sound reaches through one and sounds out a time, a moment marked.

For *Oh! there are spirits of the air* . . .

• • • •

The English distrust thought, Americans more so.

The English distrust radicals, Americans distrust aristocrats. Or used to.

Both distrust "free love."

And perhaps this distrust is not to be gainsaid for as a young polyamorist said to me, *It's so hard. You're always thinking there's someone better.*

And Shelley was always pressuring his lovers especially Mary with his often creepily complacent sexual ideology—viz. "Epipsychidion":

> True love in this differs from gold and clay,
> That to divide is not to take away.

(LL. 160–61)

For Shelley though no Mormon repeatedly created ménages
not unlike those featured in HBO's *Big Love*. Though Shel-
ley unlike that show's patriarch would welcome and even
goad his women into sleeping with other men.

For though "Love is celebrated everywhere as the sole law
which should govern the moral world" (preface to *The
Revolt of Islam*), *what is love?*

For though *the great secret of morals is Love* the question re-
mains, *what is love?*

For if "love" is *a going out of our own nature, and an identifi-
cation of ourselves with the beautiful which exists in thought,
action, or person, not our own*, one must concede that Shel-
ley too rarely went out of his own nature to reckon with the
differing natures of his lovers.

For *what is love?*

For Shelley was a sex radical.

And his doctrine of free love was exciting and costly.

For Claire Clairmont, Mary Shelley's stepsister, later reflected
on this bitterly as an old woman.

For Shelley was a feminist but within limits. For this should be
no surprise.

For *the best place for a woman in the revolution is on her back*.

For yet *Can man be free if woman be a slave?* (*The Revolt of Islam*,
Canto II, l. 1045).

•

For nevertheless he seemed to preside among angelic queer
legions when in the 1990s I joined the Chicago-based
Coalition for Positive Sexuality, a near-peer sex-educating
group whose acronym, CPS, aligned perfectly and critically
with that of the Chicago Public Schools, which at that time
had no developed sexual education curriculum.

For the motto of this group, and the title of its little green
handbook, was *Just Say Yes!*

For Nancy Reagan had said *Just Say No!*

For the drawings in the handbook were in a Socialist Realist
mode.

For its tone was militantly chirpy and the group an outgrowth
of Act Up.

For the targeted audience was teenagers and we were mainly in
our mid-to-late twenties.

For corrupting the youth of America is a lifelong project.

For queer youth were just starting to be nationally visible.

For *Just Say Yes!* could mean *Yes* to any number of things—yes
to sex with another, or others, or with yourself, or none of
the above.

For you could *Just Say Yes!* to abstinence if that was a fully
thought and felt conviction.

For why not?

For our aim was to separate *acts* from *identities*.

For *True Love Waits* was in the ascendancy.

For Eve Kosofsky Sedgwick was writing her brilliant moving
work. And Judith Butler.

For Gayle Rubin ("The Traffic in Women") and Pat Califia (*Public Sex*) and Susie Bright (*On Our Backs*) were heroes.

For our goal was to put everything on the table—condoms, dental dams, butt plugs, what have you.

For a vaginal condom was most unwieldy. As a kid said, *Is that for a horse?*

For we believed in empowerment through thought and reason and believed that young people could think and reason and sexually explore and consent in informed ways.

For as a philosophy this has problems but was an improvement over much then circulating.

For the discourse of consent is complex.

For eros does not follow reason.

For though this is true it seemed important to make sexual behavior an object of thought.

For joining CPS was one way to do that and I thank the group my compadres especially Vic Olwell and A E Murdy and Pat Chu.

For though the language of consent relies on a structure of choice—*choosing* to do or not do something—and though this language underlies disgusting consumer-models of life, & a service-economy style of sexuality, nevertheless let us recall that Milton said *reason is but choosing*.

For while safe sex is really safer sex, safer sex is worth a big shout-out.

For the discourse of abstinence had acquired an especially punitive toxic tinge in the era of AIDS.

For CPS was pro-gay, pro-woman, pro-girl, pro-sex.

For we could not distribute our pamphlets or condoms in schools.

For thus we stood on the street corners nearest high schools and did so.

For we would do this and soon a school official or a cop would come over and we would then desist if they insisted.

For the object was to disseminate information not to get arrested.

For the dissemination of information seemed and still seems part of the unfinished project of Enlightenment.

For yes repressive desublimation but still. For yes hypersexualization of the culture but still. For you know the difference.

For however inundated we are with information and however perverse the appearance of such phenomena as "infovores" still it seems a worthy thing to endorse this making available of information so minds may ponder and pivot.

For a thing once in the mind does strong work.

For Shelley was himself alert to the limits of Enlightenment even as he agitated for political reform.

For see his complicated picture of Rousseau in "The Triumph of Life" and the parade of "spoilers spoiled," including Voltaire and Kant.

For *Can he who the day before was a trampled slave suddenly become liberal-minded, forbearing, and independent?* (preface to *The Revolt of Islam*).

For he was of all English poets after Milton and Blake the one most intellectually capable of sustained critique.

For "Alastor" is one long indictment of a gifted poet's narcissism, his disappointment when he does not find a world or lover immediately responsive and adequate to his own high thoughts and desires; the poem may be read as a critique of Wordsworth but also of himself: "The Poet's self-centered seclusion was avenged by the furies of an irresistible passion pursuing him to speedy ruin" (preface to "Alastor").

And for all his flights of liberatory rhetoric he could subject his own positions to critique.

For as Maddalo (the Byron-figure) says to the Shelleyan Julian in "Julian and Maddalo": "You talk Utopia" (l. 179).

For this was no endorsement.

For Byron stuck a pin in Shelley's metaphysical afflatus and laughed Cain's doomed laugh and did not scorn to scorn.

For Shelley though often utopian wrote as much about the failure of revolutionary schemes as about their future success: see for example his anatomy of the failure of the French Revolution in *Laon and Cythna* (later revised and titled *The Revolt of Islam*).

For he was no simple *wild-eyed projector*, as Burke might have said.

For like Wordsworth he resisted the worship of "Science" and

"Reason" and "Philosophy" and "Utility" and called all that would recenter our lives in the universe "Poetry":

Poetry is indeed something divine. It is at once the centre and circumference of knowledge; it is that which comprehends all science, and that to which all science must be referred.

("A DEFENCE OF POETRY")

Poets, or those who imagine and express this indestructible order, are not only the authors of language and music, of the dance and architecture and statuary and painting: they are the institutors of laws, and the founders of civil society and the inventors of the arts of life and the teachers . . .

("A DEFENCE OF POETRY")

We have more moral, political and historical wisdom, than we know how to reduce into practise; we have more scientific and œconomical knowledge than can be accommodated to the just distribution of the produce which it multiplies . . . We want the creative faculty to imagine that which we know; we want the generous impulse to act that which we imagine; we want the poetry of life: our calculations have outrun conception; we have eaten more than we can digest.

("A DEFENCE OF POETRY")

For he wrote against the vulgar ideology of progress and saw how technological advances left supposedly advanced peoples still grossly tyrannized & unequal, their populations groaning—

For he saw that *man, having enslaved the elements, remains himself a slave* ("A Defence of Poetry").

• • • •

For Shelley is a fragment.

For editing him has been a contentious world of work for two centuries.

For Shelley's father prohibited Mary Shelley from publishing the Collected Poems she wanted to soon after Shelley's death.

For see among other sources *Shelley's Ghost: Reshaping the Image of a Literary Family*, by Stephen Hebron and Elizabeth C. Denlinger.

For Mary Shelley later overhauled the *Posthumous Poems* of 1824 when she published Shelley's *Poetical Works* in 1839. There in her notes to the poems she snuck in a kind of shadow biography of Shelley, idealized and somewhat pacified but still radical, though Mary did not fully restore the atheistical passages of *Queen Mab*—passages that would have outraged public opinion and the still-living Sir Timothy Shelley, and which still disquieted eminent Victorians, and would even now win no friends among Tea Partiers.

For later Shelley's only surviving child Percy Florence Shelley
and his wife Lady Jane Shelley further Victorianized Shel-
ley making him safe for drawing rooms.

Thus the insipid version of Shelley one typically gets from
anthologies.

For his last poem "The Triumph of Life" was left unfinished;
and Paul de Man wrote an astonishing essay, "Shelley Dis-
figured," about the status of Shelley's forcibly yet involun-
tarily broken-off poem and his forcibly yet involuntarily
broken-off life.

"Then what is life? I cried."—

is how one version of "The Triumph of Life" ends.

The version Mary Shelley published in 1824. The version as
well in her 1839 *Collected.*

This was the version I first read, in the Modern Library edi-
tion of *John Keats and Percy Bysshe Shelley: Complete Poeti-
cal Works, with the Explanatory Notes of Shelley's Poems by
Mrs. Shelley.*

"Then what is life? I cried."—

the question, the exclamatory verb, the period, the fatally sus-
pended dash—

This is my favorite version.

There are things to be said for other editions of the poem, not
least the scholarly version published in Donald H. Reiman

and Sharon B. Powers's Norton Critical Edition of *Shelley's Poetry and Prose*, and in Reiman and Neil Fraistat's second edition of the Norton:

> "Then what is life?" I said . . . the cripple cast
> His eye upon the car which now had rolled
> Onward, as if that look must be the last,
>
> And answered . . . "Happy those for whom the fold
> Of

The fold / Of
?
[Happy those . . .]

> *Then what is life? I cried.—*

• • • •

For Shelley is the future.

For Shelley is the time-of-the-now.

For one might say of him what Mandelstam wrote of Dante: "It is unthinkable to read the cantos of Dante without aiming them in the direction of the present day. They were made for that. They are missiles for capturing the future" ("Conversation about Dante").

For Shelley is an Italian poet in English.

For his "Triumph of Life" is the most astounding transposition into English of Dante's terza rima.

For his only surviving child was named *Percy Florence Shelley*.

For he died in the Gulf of Spezia which partly because of his fame is now known as the Golfo dei Poeti.

For Shelley was always sailing off.

For this is true literally and metaphorically.

For Shelley did not observe the difference.

For he imagines himself sailing after the transfigured Keats in "Adonais"—

> my spirit's bark is driven,
> Far from the shore, far from the trembling throng
> Whose sails were never to the tempest given;
> The massy earth and sphèrèd skies are riven!
> I am borne darkly, fearfully, afar;
>
> (LL. 488–92)

—his little skiff, his "spirit's bark," echoing Dante's *barca* in the *Paradiso*.

Shelley drowned near the Golfo Paradiso on the Ligurian Coast.

Carried on a bark to the abode where the eternal are—

Carried in the immortals' car.

For Shelley is a vehicle.

For Shelley is a medium.

He played *the soul's giant harp* (passages canceled from "Epi-
   psychidion").
He was rung by the wind.
He was blown by the wind and the wind in the end blew him
   dead.
His *silver lyre unstrung* ("Adonais," l. 324).
Water wind and sail and a dead poet.
Yet has he not *outsoared the shadow of our night*? ("Adonais,"
   l. 352).
For he wrote of *the enamoured air* ("Triumph of Life," l. 39) and
   his work enamors the air.
For *my soul was an enchanted boat*—
For in the enamored air I enamored learned to sail with a love
   whose name in Italian is the air.
For

> By thee, most beautiful of pilots,
>
> Where never mortal pinnace glided,
>
> the boat of my desire is guided—
>
> (*PROMETHEUS UNBOUND*, II.V.92–94)

For *yet all love is sweet, / Given or returned* (*Prometheus Unbound*,
   II.v.39–40)—and sweetest that given and returned.
For perhaps *we are all Greeks* especially those who know Greek.
For he is both vatic and intellectual; the vatic sometimes bests
   him but also bears him *fearfully afar*, to his highest and best
   pitch—

For yes he is of that *Visionary Company* as Harold Bloom said—
For

> The One remains, the many change and pass;
> Heaven's light forever shines, Earth's shadows fly;
> Life, like a dome of many-coloured glass,
> Stains the white radiance of Eternity,
> Until Death tramples it to fragments . . .
>
> ("ADONAIS," LL. 460–64)

For he knew

> The great secret of morals is Love; or a going out of our own
> nature, and an identification of ourselves with the beautiful
> which exists in thought, action, or person, not our own.
>
> ("A DEFENCE OF POETRY")

For though he is endlessly disappointing, as so many idealists
and idealizers are,

> Let us for a moment stoop to the arbitration of popular
> breath, and usurping and uniting in our own persons the in-
> compatible characters of accuser, witness, judge and execu-
> tioner, let us decide without trial, testimony, or form, that
> certain motives of those who are "there sitting where we
> dare not soar" are reprehensible. Let us assume that Homer
> was a drunkard, that Virgil was a flatterer, that Horace was

a coward, that Tasso was a madman, that Lord Bacon was a peculator, that Raphael was a libertine, that Spenser was a poet laureate.

("A DEFENCE OF POETRY")

Let us concede with Shelley that

The persons in whom this [poetical] power resides, may often, as regards many portions of their nature, have little apparent correspondence with that spirit of good of which they are the ministers.

("A DEFENCE OF POETRY")

Let us admit we do not know if, as he insisted, "[t]heir errors have been weighed and found to have been dust in the balance": whether "they have been washed in the blood of the mediator and the redeemer Time"—

Let us remember the tears and the anguish and the corpses—

But let us say too that "Life, and the world, or whatever we call that which we are and feel, is an astonishing thing" ("On Life," 1819).

Let him astonish us, that *astonishing thing* still ringing in *the enamoured air.*

15

MY POETS II

AN ENVOI IN THE FORM OF A CENTO

O what an endlesse worke have I in hand![1]
For I, that God of Loves servantz serve,
Ne dar to Love, for myn unlyklinesse, / Preyen for speed, [2]
And anyway except in daily life nobody is anybody.[3]
I don't know how many souls I have.[4]
Since in a net I seek to hold the wind[5]
I am, til God me bettre mynde sende, / At dulcarnoun.[6]
I wish that I might be a thinking stone.[7]
What to make of a diminished thing.[8]

1. Edmund Spenser, *Fairie Queene*, Book 4, Canto XII, stanza 1.

2. Geoffrey Chaucer, *Troilus and Criseyde*, Book 1, 15–17.

3. Gertrude Stein, *Everybody's Autobiography*.

4. Fernando Pessoa, "I don't know how many souls I have," trans. Richard Zenith.

5. Thomas Wyatt, "Whoso List to Hunt."

6. Chaucer, *Troilus and Criseyde*, Book 3, 930–31.

7. Wallace Stevens, "Le Monocle de Mon Oncle."

8. Robert Frost, "Oven Bird."

Not this. What then?[9]

Is the year only lost to me?[10]

Who, if I cried out, would hear me among the angels' /
hierarchies?[11]

Think not of them, thou hast thy music too.[12]

But is the / earth as full as life was full, of them?[13]

I too felt the curious abrupt questionings stir within me:[14]

Who are these coming to the sacrifice?[15]

Whence are we, and why are we? of what scene / The actors or
spectators?[16]

Was it for this / That one, the fairest of all Rivers, loved

To blend his murmurs with my Nurse's song?[17]

"Then what is life?" I cried—[18]

9. Ron Silliman, *Tjanting*.

10. George Herbert, "The Collar."

11. Rainer Maria Rilke, *Duino Elegies*, The First Elegy, trans. Stephen
Mitchell.

12. John Keats, "To Autumn."

13. Frank O'Hara, "A Step Away from Them."

14. Walt Whitman, "Crossing Brooklyn Ferry."

15. John Keats, "Ode on a Grecian Urn."

16. Percy Bysshe Shelley, "Adonais."

17. William Wordsworth, *The Prelude*, I, 271–73.

18. Shelley, "The Triumph of Life."

While my hair was still cut straight across my forehead[19]
I struck the board, and cried, "No more! / I will abroad!"[20]
Let us go, through certain half-deserted streets[21]
Magick'd in the Candle's Glow[22]
At five in the afternoon:[23]
Have we not stood here like trees in the ground long enough?[24]
O that a chariot of cloud were mine![25]
O for a horse with wings![26]
The light foot hears you and the brightness begins:[27]
O body swayed to music, O brightening glance—[28]
Love hath no fire but what he steals from her bright eyes.[29]
I, now thirty-seven years old in perfect health begin.[30]

19. Ezra Pound, "The River-Merchant's Wife: A Letter."

20. George Herbert, "The Collar."

21. T. S. Eliot, "The Love Song of J. Alfred Prufrock."

22. August Kleinzahler, "Balling at 50."

23. Federico García Lorca, "Lament for Ignacio Sánchez Mejías," trans. Donald Merriam and W. S. Merwin.

24. Whitman, "Passage to India."

25. Shelley, "Fragment of a Song (O That a Chariot of Cloud Were Mine!)."

26. Shakespeare, *Cymbeline*, Act 3, Scene 2.

27. Robert Duncan, "A Poem Beginning with a Line from Pindar."

28. William Butler Yeats, "Among School Children."

29. Thomas Campion (attrib.), "When Laura Smiles."

30. Whitman, "Song of Myself," section 1.

I'm beginning to know myself. I don't exist.[31]

'Tis strange the mind, that very fiery particle![32]

I, so given to indolence, so easily bored:[33]

I have had to learn the simplest things / last:[34]

I am I because my little dog knows me;[35]

I know a little language of my cat;[36]

A white hunter is nearly crazy.[37]

I have tried to be accurate in this description / in case
    someone else should follow me.[38]

I am not Prince Hamlet.[39]

I am no Greek, hath not th'advantage.[40]

"i" wants to be a man like marjorie perloff, helen hennessy
    vendler, boris tomashevsky.[41]

    31. Pessoa (Álvaro de Campos), "I'm beginning to know myself. I don't exist," trans. Richard Zenith.

    32. George Gordon, Lord Byron, *Don Juan*, Canto XI, stanza 60.

    33. Pessoa (Álvaro de Campos), "Salutation to Walt Whitman," trans. Richard Zenith.

    34. Charles Olson, "Maximus, to himself."

    35. Stein, "Identity a Poem."

    36. Duncan, "A Little Language."

    37. Stein, *Tender Buttons*.

    38. Louise Glück, "Landscape."

    39. Eliot, "The Love Song of J. Alfred Prufrock."

    40. Olson, "The Kingfishers."

    41. Olena Kalytiak Davis, "The Lyric 'I' Drives to Pick Up Her Children from School: A Poem in the Postconfessional Mode."

I know not what to do. My mind is divided.[42]
I sing to use the Waiting.[43]

Here is no question of whiteness.[44]
I have stained the sun with my black love:[45]
It is only because I have interested myself / in what was slain in
    the sun.[46]
I made my soul familiar— / with her extremity.[47]
The sun set in the sea; the same odd sun
rose from the sea, / and there was one of it and one of me.[48]
When shall I come to say of the sun / It is a sea, it shares nothing,[49]
thigh and tongue, beloved, are heavy with it.[50]
This is not exactly what I mean / Any more than the sun is the
    sun.[51]
I wonder what Adam and Eve / think of it by this time.[52]

42. H.D./Sappho, "Fragment 36."

43. Dickinson, "I sing to use the Waiting" (955).

44. William Carlos Williams, "Queen-Anne's Lace."

45. Osip Mandelstam, from *Tristia*, trans. Clarence Brown and W. S.
Merwin.

46. Olson, "The Kingfishers."

47. Emily Dickinson, "I read my sentence—steadily—" (432).

48. Elizabeth Bishop, "Crusoe in England."

49. Stevens, "The Man with the Blue Guitar," stanza VII.

50. Denise Levertov, "The Ache of Marriage."

51. Laura (Riding) Jackson, "The World and I."

52. Marianne Moore, "Marriage."

No more shall grief of mine the season wrong.[53]

Now I will do nothing but listen.[54]

Have we not darken'd and dazed ourselves with books long
    enough?[55]

O we can wait no longer, / We too take ship O soul—[56]

My soul is an enchanted boat[57]

and I am little short of dying.[58]

Why linger, why turn back, why shrink, my Heart?[59]

Should we have stayed at home and thought of here?[60]

The spangled sea below wants me to fall.[61]

How odd the Girl's life looks

Behind this soft Eclipse![62]

God gives us Women[63]

Between mountains, woods, abysses, / A paradise of
    wildernesses![64]

53. William Wordsworth, "Ode: Intimations of Immortality."

54. Whitman, "Song of Myself," section 26.

55. Whitman, "Passage to India," section 9.

56. Whitman, "Passage to India," section 8.

57. Shelley, *Prometheus Unbound*.

58. Sappho, "Fragment 31."

59. Shelley, "Adonais."

60. Elizabeth Bishop, "Questions of Travel."

61. Bishop, "The Unbeliever."

62. Dickinson, "I'm 'wife'—I've finished that—" (225).

63. Dickinson, "Title divine, is mine" (194).

64. Shelley, *Prometheus Unbound*.

If sex were all,[65]

My name is Fred Seidel[66]

And the running blackberry would adorn the parlors of heaven.[67]

Cold dark deep and absolutely clear,[68]

My mind's not right.[69]

O the mind, mind has mountains.[70]

Psychology which explains everything / explains nothing / and
    we are still in doubt.[71]

The Pansy at my feet / Doth the same tale repeat:[72]

I am an indicated other.[73]

Position is where you / put it, where it is,[74]

where the dry blood talks

where the old appetite walks[75]

I saw the first pear / As it fell.[76]

65. Stevens, "Le Monocle de Mon Oncle," stanza XI.

66. Frederick Seidel, "Home."

67. Whitman, "Song of Myself," section 31.

68. Bishop, "At the Fishhouses."

69. Robert Lowell, "Skunk Hour."

70. Gerard Manley Hopkins, "No Worst, There is none. Pitched past
pitch of grief."

71. Moore, "Marriage."

72. Wordsworth, "Ode: Intimations of Immortality"

73. (Riding) Jackson, "I Am."

74. Robert Creeley, "The Window."

75. Olson, "The Kingfishers."

76. H.D., "Orchard."

It has no Future—but itself.[77]

But there is fruit / and thou hast hands.[78]

A pious wish to whiteness gone over[79]

Makes my brain blind—[80]

I sing the body electric,[81]

the darker, accurate rose of sex[82]

until the whole field is a / white desire.[83]

Green I love you green (verde te quiero verde)[84]

and I am greener than grass . . .[85]

So let me be thy choir.[86]

Just as you feel when you look on the river and sky, so I felt.[87]

Oh! there are Spirits of the Air![88]

Hang it all, Robert Browning,[89]

77. Dickinson, "Pain—has an Element of Blank—" (760).

78. Herbert, "The Collar."

79. Williams, "Queen-Anne's Lace."

80. H.D., "Fragment 36."

81. Whitman, "I Sing the Body Electric."

82. Bishop, "Vague Poem."

83. Williams, "Queen-Anne's Lace."

84. Lorca, "Romance Sonámbulo."

85. Sappho, "Fragment 31."

86. Keats, "Ode to Psyche."

87. Whitman, "Crossing Brooklyn Ferry," section 3.

88. Shelley, "Oh! there are spirits of the air."

89. Pound, *The Cantos*, Canto II.

The poet is a radio. The poet is a liar.

The poet is a counterpunching radio.[90]

He is callèd by thy name[91]

And what I assume you shall assume.[92]

O you who looking within the mirror discover

in gratitude how common, how lawful your / desire,[93]

You know that I am You, and you are happy about it![94]

The city is out there, and you / are a citizen—What's / your
   report?[95]

Is this then a touch? quivering me to a new identity—[96]

I'm Czar—I'm "Woman" now.[97]

You are of course never yourself.[98]

Of course, it is strange to inhabit the earth no longer[99]

with rocks, and stones, and trees.[100]

Strange to no longer desire one's desires.[101]

90. Jack Spicer, "Sporting Life."

91. Blake, "The Lamb."

92. Whitman, "Song of Myself," section 1.

93. Frank Bidart, "The Second Hour of the Night."

94. Pessoa (Álvaro de Campos), "Salutation to Walt Whitman," trans.
Richard Zenith.

95. Eleni Sikelianos, "Monster Lives of Boys and Girls."

96. Whitman, "Song of Myself," section 28.

97. Dickinson, "I'm 'wife'—I've finished that—" (225).

98. Stein, *Everybody's Autobiography*.

99. Rilke, *Duino Elegies*, First Elegy.

100. Wordsworth, "A Slumber Did My Spirit Seal."

101. Rilke, *Duino Elegies*, First Elegy.

The face of every one / That passes by me is a mystery.[102]

The future is a faded song,[103]

Song of the bleeding throat.[104]

I heard words / and words full / of holes / aching.[105]

Can you make it out / Almost a hiss / An old shellac LP of white noise—[106]

O vast Rondure, swimming in space[107]

Fled is that music:—Do I wake or sleep?[108]

102. Wordsworth, *Prelude* VII, 596–97.
103. Eliot, "Dry Salvages," III, *Four Quartets*.
104. Whitman, "When Lilacs Last in the Dooryard Bloom'd."
105. Creeley, "The Language."
106. Kleinzahler, "Hyper-Berceuse, 3 A.M."
107. Whitman, "Passage to India," section 5.
108. Keats, "Ode to a Nightingale."

WORKS CONSULTED OR REMEMBERED AND FURTHER READING

FOR "MY CHAUCER/KANKEDORT"

Chaucer, Geoffrey. *The Riverside Chaucer*, 3rd ed. General editor Larry D. Benson, based on the edition by F. N. Robinson. New York: Oxford University Press, 1987.

FOR "MY IMPASSES: ON NOT BEING ABLE TO READ POETRY"

The Postmoderns: The New American Poetry Revised. Edited by Donald Allen and George F. Butterick. New York: Grove Press, 1982.

FOR "MY ELIZABETH BISHOP/ (MY GERTRUDE STEIN)"

Bishop, Elizabeth. *The Complete Poems, 1927–1979*. New York. Farrar, Straus and Giroux, 1987.

———. *Poems*. New York: Farrar, Straus and Giroux, 2011.

———. *Prose*. Edited by Lloyd Schwartz. New York: Farrar, Straus and Giroux, 2011.

———. *Edgar Allan Poe & The Juke-Box: Uncollected Poems, Drafts, and Fragments*. Edited by Alice Quinn. New York: Farrar, Straus and Giroux, 2006.

Bishop, Elizabeth, and Robert Lowell. *Words in Air: The Complete Correspondence Between Elizabeth Bishop and Robert Lowell*. Edited by Thomas Travisano with Saskia Hamilton. New York: Farrar, Straus and Giroux, 2008.

Lowell, Robert. *Collected Poems*. Edited by Frank Bidart and David Gewanter. New York: Farrar, Straus and Giroux, 2003.

Stein, Gertrude. *Everybody's Autobiography*. New York: Random House, 1937. Reprint, Cambridge, MA: Exact Change/Random House, 1993.

FOR "MY WALLACE STEVENS"

Stevens, Wallace. *Wallace Stevens: Collected Poetry and Prose*. Edited by Frank Kermode and Joan Richardson. New York: Library of America, 1997.

FOR "MY WILLIAM CARLOS WILLIAMS"

Notley, Alice. *Mysteries of Small Houses*. New York: Penguin, 1998.

Williams, William Carlos. *In the American Grain*. New York: New Directions, 1956.

———. *Paterson*. New York: New Directions, 1963.

———. *Spring and All*. 1923. New York: New Directions, 2011.

FOR "MY MARIANNE MOORE"

Moore, Marianne. *The Poems of Marianne Moore*. Edited by Grace Schulman. New York: Viking, 2003.

FOR "MY H.D."

Arendt, Hannah. *The Human Condition*. Chicago: University of Chicago Press, 1989.

———. *On Revolution*. New York: Penguin, 1990.

Benveniste, Emile. "Subjectivity in Language." 1958. In *Problems in General Linguistics*. Translated by Mary Elizabeth Meek. Coral Gables, FL: University of Miami Press, 1971. Paperback ed. 1997.

Carson, Anne. *If Not, Winter: Fragments of Sappho*. New York: Knopf, 2002.

Greek Lyric: Sappho and Alcaeus. Edited and translated by David

A. Campbell. The Loeb Classical Library. Cambridge, MA: Harvard University Press, 1982.

H.D. *Collected Poems, 1912–1944*. Edited by Louis L. Martz. New York: New Directions, 1983.

———. *Notes on Thought and Vision and The Wise Sappho*. With an introduction by Albert Gelpi. San Francisco: City Lights Books, 1982.

———. *Tribute to Freud*. With a foreword by Norman Holmes Person. New York: New Directions, 1974.

Sappho: The Poetry of Sappho. Translated by Jim Powell. New York: Oxford University Press, 2007.

Scarry, Elaine. *The Body in Pain: The Making and Unmaking of the World*. New York: Oxford University Press, 1985.

Stewart, Susan. *Poetry and the Fate of the Senses*. Chicago: University of Chicago Press, 2002.

FOR "MY LOUISE GLÜCK"

Badiou, Alain. "Fifteen Theses on Contemporary Art." In *Lacanian Ink* 23. www.lacan.com/frameXXIII7.htm.

Glück, Louise. *Averno*. New York: Farrar, Straus and Giroux, 2006.

———. *The First Four Books of Poems*. New York: Ecco Press, 1999.

———. *Meadowlands*. New York: Ecco Press, 2001.

———. *Proofs and Theories: Essays on Poetry*. New York: Ecco Press, 1994.

———. *The Wild Iris*. New York: Ecco Press, 1992.

Schiller, Friedrich. *Naive and Sentimental Poetry and On the Sublime: Two Essays*. Translated and with an introduction and notes by Julius A. Elias. New York: Frederick Ungar, 1966.

FOR "MY FANNY HOWE"

Howe, Fanny. *Alsace-Lorraine*. Telephone Books Press, 1982.
———. *Selected Poems*. Berkeley: University of California Press, 2000.

FOR "MY EMILY DICKINSON/ *MY EMILY DICKINSON*"

Faludi, Susan. *The Terror Dream: Fear and Fantasy in Post-9/11 America*. New York: Metropolitan Books, 2007.
Howe, Susan. *My Emily Dickinson*. With a preface by Eliot Weinberger. New York: New Directions, 2007.
The Poems of Emily Dickinson. Reading ed. Edited by R. W. Franklin. Cambridge, MA: Belknap Press of Harvard University, 1999.

FOR "MY SHELLEY/(MY ROMANTICS)"

Bloom, Harold. "The Internalization of Quest-Romance." In *Romanticism and Consciousness: Essays in Criticism*. Edited by Harold Bloom. New York: Norton, 1970, 3–24.

de Man, Paul. *The Rhetoric of Romanticism*. New York: Columbia University Press, 1984.

Eliot, T. S. *The Use of Poetry and the Use of Criticism: Studies in the Relation of Poetry to Criticism in England*. London: Faber and Faber, 1933.

Hay, Daisy. *Young Romantics: The Shelleys, Byron, and Other Tangled Lives*. New York: Farrar, Straus and Giroux, 2010.

Hebron, Stephen, and Elizabeth C. Denlinger. *Shelley's Ghost: Reshaping the Image of a Literary Family*. Oxford: University of Oxford, Bodleian Library, 2010.

Holmes, Richard. *Shelley: The Pursuit*. New York: New York Review of Books, 2003.

John Keats and Percy Bysshe Shelley: Complete Poetical Works, with the Explanatory Notes of Shelley's Poems by Mrs. Shelley. New York: Modern Library, n.d.

Shelley's Poetry and Prose. Selected and edited by Donald H. Reiman and Neil Fraistat. New York: Norton, 2002.

Wroe, Ann. *Being Shelley: The Poet's Search for Himself*. London: Jonathan Cape, 2007.

AMBIENT STUFF/SPIRITS IN THE AIR

Barrett, Ed. ALL, including *Bosston* (Boston: Pressed Wafer, 2008), *Kevin White* (Pressed Wafer, 2007), and *Rub Out* (Pressed Wafer, 2004).

Bidart, Frank. ALL, including *Desire: Poems* (New York: Farrar, Straus and Giroux, 1999); *In the Western Night: Collected Poems, 1965–1990* (Farrar, Straus and Giroux, 1991); and *Star Dust: Poems* (Farrar, Straus and Giroux: 2006).

Carson, Anne. ALL, including *Autobiography of Red* (New York: Vintage, 1999); *The Beauty of the Husband* (Vintage, 2002); *Eros the Bittersweet* (Princeton: Princeton University Press, 1986); and *Glass, Irony, and God* (New York: New Directions, 1995).

Christensen, Inger. ALL, including *Alphabet*, translated by Susanna Nied (New York: New Directions, 2011), and *It*, translated by Susanna Nied (New Directions, 2006).

Coleridge's Poetry and Prose. Selected and edited by Nicholas Halmi, Paul Magnuson, and Raimonda Modiano. New York: Norton, 2004.

Corbett, William. ALL, including *Opening Day* (Brooklyn, NY: Hanging Loose Press, 2008) and *The Whalen Poem* (Hanging Loose Press, 2011).

Fisher, Roy. ALL, including *Selected Poems* (Chicago: Flood Editions, 2011).

Hoover, Paul, ed. *Postmodern American Poetry: A Norton Anthology*. New York: Norton, 1994.

Johnston, Devin. ALL, including *Sources* (New York: Turtle Point Press, 2008); *Telepathy* (Brooklyn, N.S.W., Australia: Paper Bark Press, 2002); and *Traveler* (New York: Farrar, Straus and Giroux, 2011).

Kleinzahler, August. ALL, including *Sleeping It Off in Rapid City:*

Poems, New and Selected (New York: Farrar, Straus and Giroux, 2008) and *The Strange Hours Travelers Keep* (Farrar, Straus and Giroux, 2004).

Leopardi, Giacomo. *Canti: Poems / A Bilingual Edition*. Translated by Jonathan Galassi. New York: Farrar, Straus and Giroux, 2010.

Mandelstam, Osip. *The Selected Poems of Osip Mandelstam*. Translated by Clarence Brown and W. S. Merwin. New York: New York Review of Books, 1973, 2004.

Montale, Eugenio. *Collected Poems, 1920–1954: Revised Bilingual Edition*. Translated by Jonathan Galassi. New York: Farrar, Straus and Giroux, 2000.

Muldoon, Paul. ALL, including *Hay: Poems* (New York: Farrar, Straus and Giroux, 1999), *Horse Latitudes: Poems* (Farrar, Straus and Giroux, 2007), and *Moy Sand and Gravel: Poems* (Farrar, Straus and Giroux, 2002).

The Norton Anthology of Modern and Contemporary Poetry. Edited by Jahan Ramazani, Richard Ellman, and Robert O'Clair. New York: Norton, 2003. 2 vols.

The Norton Anthology of Poetry. 5th ed. Edited by Margaret Ferguson, Mary Jo Salter, and Jon Stallworthy. New York: Norton, 2005.

Peterson, Katie. *This One Tree*. Kalamazoo, MI: New Issues, 2006.

Phillips, Adam. "In Praise of Difficult Children." *London Review of Books* 31, no. 3 (February 12, 2009).

Pickard, Tom. ALL, including *Ballad of Jamie Allan* (Chicago:

Flood Editions, 2007) and *The Dark Months of May* (Flood Editions, 2004).

Pound, Ezra. *Literary Essays*. New York: New Directions, 1968.

———. *Selected Prose, 1909–1965*. New York: New Directions, 1973.

Robertson, Lisa. *The Weather*. Vancouver, BC: New Star Books, 2001.

Seidel, Frederick. *Poems 1959–2009*. New York: Farrar, Straus and Giroux, 2009.

Slatkin, Laura. *The Power of Thetis and Selected Essays*. Cambridge, MA: Center for Hellenic Studies, Harvard University, 2011.

Whitman, Walt. *Complete Poetry and Selected Prose*. Edited by James E. Miller, Jr. Boston: Houghton Mifflin, 1959.

Wordsworth, William. *The Prelude: 1799, 1805, 1850*. Edited by M. H. Abrams, Stephen Gill, and Jonathan Wordsworth. New York: Norton, 1979

———. *The Prelude, or Growth of a Poet's Mind*. 1805. Edited by Ernest de Sélincourt. New York: Oxford University Press, 1942.

———. *The Thirteen Book Prelude*. Edited by Mark L. Reed. Ithaca, NY: Cornell University Press, 1991.

Wordsworth, William, and Samuel Taylor Coleridge. *Lyrical Ballads*. Edited by R. L. Brett and A. R. Jones. New York: Routledge, 1991.

MY ACKNOWLEDGMENTS

Thank you Mom and Dad for song and story and the crucial world-welcome.

Thank you Michael McLane and Colleen Mullen for solidarity throughout—and Meredith, Micheal, Darcy, Bridget, Liam, and Sitota for ever-expanding circles.

Thank you Peter Schwartz for giving me *The Selected Poetry of Rainer Maria Rilke*, edited and translated by Stephen Mitchell. Thank you for though I did not read this book right away I later did and often.

Thank you Janice Knight for Elizabeth Bishop's *Complete Poems*. And thank you John Farrell for supervising my thesis even though it was not at all postmodern.

Thank you Erik S. for Joseph Brodsky's *To Urania* and much else.

Thank you New Directions for your H.D., Ezra Pound, William Carlos Williams, and other bang-up modernists and your current crew, and thank you City Lights and always Lawrence Ferlinghetti.

Thank you Eliot Weinberger for all ventures and for *What I Heard About Iraq*.

Thank you Elizabeth Taylor for commissioning essays on poetry thus encouraging wide reading and also a hope for resonances in the world; and thank you for profound friendship and generosity. Thank you *Chicago Tribune*.

Thank you Carole Slatkin for solidarity, for birds, and much else; and thank you Robin Brown, ace photographer. And thank you Amy Johnson.

Thank you Norton for your vexed and magisterial tomes.

Thank you Jerome Rothenberg for your imaginative, synoptic anthologies.

Thank you Douglas Messerli for Sun & Moon and Green Integer and your anthologies.

Thank you William Corbett for Pressed Wafer and all galvanic efforts and Beantown camaraderie. And thank you Ed Barrett (Monsignor) and Fanny Howe.

Thank you Beverly Corbett, maîtresse de cuisine, for endless hospitality.

Thank you Askold Melnyczuk for Arrowsmith Press and thank you Alex Johnson.

Thank you *Chicago Review* especially former editors Angela Sorby, David Nicholls, and Andrew Rathmann for providing an oasis in a cold desert.

Thank you *Boston Review* especially editors Deborah Chasman and Joshua Cohen for ditto.

Thank you editors and translators of the Loeb Classical Library.

Thank you Bruce King for divagations poetic and otherwise.

Thank you Brighde Mullins for recommending Inger Christensen's work.

Thank you Lawrence Joseph for Gertrude Stein's *Everybody's Autobiography*.

Thank you Flood Editions Devin Johnston and Michael O'Leary for many things not least bringing Tom Pickard and Roy Fisher to a U.S. readership.

Thank you Tom Pickard for jumpstarting Basil Bunting.

Thank you Northern Irish poets for dynamizing poetry in the U.K. And thank you Scots. And thank you for not being offended by the term "U.K."

Thank you Bloodaxe Books for vigorous English poetry.

Thank you Paper Bark Press Robert Adamson and Juno Gemes for antipodean revelations.

Thank you Small Press Distribution.

Thank you editors of fine magazines and journals and books, who supported this and other work: David Baker, *Kenyon Review*; Rob Casper, Cathy Park Hong, and Evie Shockley, *jubilat*; Deborah Chasman, Joshua Cohen, Timothy Donnelly, and Benjamin Paloff, *Boston Review*; Robyn Creswell and Lorin Stein, *The Paris Review*; Bart Eeckhout and Lisa Goldfarb, *The Wallace Stevens Journal*; Brigid Hughes, *A Public Space*; Brantly Martin and Valentina Ilardi Martin, *Grey*; Paul Muldoon, *The New Yorker*; Molly McQuade, *One Word: Contemporary Writers on the*

Words They Love or Loathe; and Don Selby and Diane Boller, *Poetry Daily*.

Thank you Robyn Creswell for readerly acuity and generosity, and thank you Sara Bershtel, Elizabeth Denlinger, Jeff Dolven, Langdon Hammer, and August Kleinzahler.

Thank you MacDowell Colony heaven-haven which supported the writing of *My Poets*.

Thank you Rachel Berchten and Rebecca Wells (University of California Press), Sara Bershtel and Mimi Ross (Metropolitan/Holt), Kelsey Ford (New Directions), Victoria Fox (FSG), Christine Lee (Simon & Schuster), Peter London (Ecco/Harper Collins), Sam Moore and Jeffery Corrick (Penguin), Jennifer Rowley (Random House), Robert Sharrard (City Lights), and Judith Wilburn (Harvard University Press) for your gracious shepherding through the thicket of permissions.

Thank you Miranda Popkey for heroic attentiveness and thank you angelic legions of FSG.

Thank you Nayon Cho and Jeff Clark (again!) for envisionings.

Thank you Julia Targ for all furtherings.

Thank you Jonathan Galassi *eagle spirit* without whom no *My Poets*.

Thank you Laura *delicate spirit* without whom no this poet.

PERMISSIONS
ACKNOWLEDGMENTS